A signed message from the author:

I am delighted to personally sign this copy of my book for you. It is the first work on scripophily, the collecting of Old Bonds and Share certificates, and I hope that it will provide you with an enlightening introduction to this fascinating subject.

Whether you approach it as an area of investment of purely for aesthetic and decorative appeal I hope that my book will interest and enthuse you.

Keith Hollender

SCRIPOPHILY

State of Bahia (Brazil), £100 bond of 1913.

Jacket pictures: The front cover shows a $1,000 bond of the Boston Hartford and Erie Rail Road issued in 1866. On the back is a Banque Industrielle de Chine bearer share.

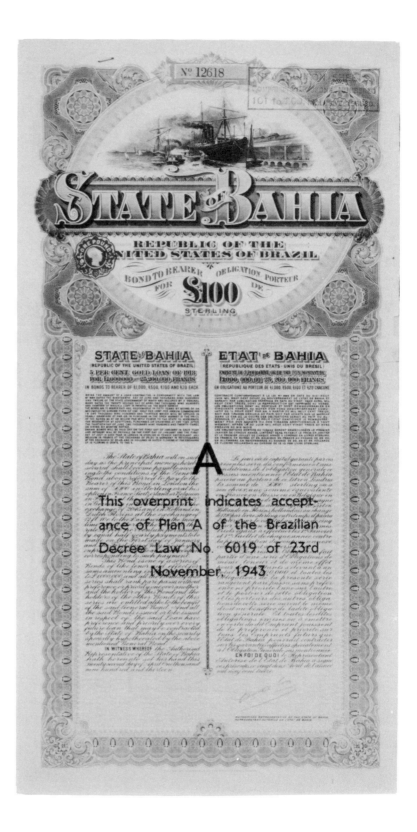

SCRIPOPHILY

Collecting Bonds and Share Certificates

Keith Hollender

WARD LOCK LIMITED · LONDON

TO THE MEMORY OF MY FATHER

© Ward Lock Limited 1982

First published in Great Britain in 1982
by Ward Lock Limited, 82 Gower Street,
London WC1E 6EQ, a Pentos Company.

Designed by Viv Harper
House editor Suzanne Kendall
Text filmset in Garamond

Printed and bound in Great Britain by
M & A Thomson Litho Ltd, East Kilbride, Scotland

British Library Cataloguing in Publication Data

Hollender, Keith
    Scripophily: collecting bond and share certificates.
    1. Bonds – Collectors and collecting
    2. Stock certificates – Collectors and collecting
    I. Title
    769.5   HG4651

    ISBN 0–7063–6155–5

Acknowledgments

In addition to the invaluable information drawn from
publications listed in the bibliography, grateful thanks
are due to Leila Kay for devotion to the typewriter,
Tim Barker for great assistance on the Russian railway
section and Veronica for continuous support. Thanks
are also due to The Bond and Share Society for their
helpful advice and information and to R. M. Smythe &
Co., Herzog Hollender Phillips & Co., and E. H.
Morton for the loan of items for photography.

                  Keith Hollender

CONTENTS

INTRODUCTION

For many of you, picking up this book is probably your first encounter with scripophily. Hopefully it was not located in the medical section; the adopted word for the hobby of collecting old bond and share certificates is more than a little off-putting but the implication of 'something catching' is perhaps not wholly out of place, for the hobby itself certainly *is* catching and we hope you will enjoy being caught.

Solely devoted to the subject of scripophily, this book is designed to introduce the newcomer to the hobby as well as enthuse existing collectors. The emphasis, so far as collecting themes is concerned, has been firmly placed on the economic history behind these fascinating documents. The author sees this aspect as the most important positive aspect of the subject which in many ways offers the collector at heart (and possibly not since schooldays) a *sophisticated* hobby.

The book has been split into three main sections: General background and history, Collecting themes, and Developing a collection. The appendices provide additional information on dealers, auction houses and societies. The very newness of the subject highlights research opportunities, which, it is hoped, will be as appealing to the new collector as the bonds themselves. But before starting Part 1 it may be appropriate to say something on the subject of investment. For many years now much of the appeal of collecting, whether it be antiques, vintage cars or stamps, has been fired by thoughts of future monetary gain. Such thinking has been encouraged by both dealers and auction houses keen to tap huge investment funds. Indeed, there are many instances where individuals have made substantial capital gains over very short periods in all collecting fields – on the other hand, other speculations, often made by the unknowledgeable, have seriously backfired and equally large losses have resulted.

Collecting simply for reasons of investment is a field best left to the experts and, although it is the intention of this book to provide expert knowledge to the scripophilist, we strongly advise against such a reason for collecting. Those deciding to start a collection, in whatever field, should primarily do so because of a personal interest in the subject itself – if after a number of years, for reasons of rarity and demand, that collection acquires a premium value, then that should be seen as a bonus and not a justification of the original decision. Of course it is an undeniable fact that items genuinely produced in a past age are irreplaceable no matter how much modern technology develops. Many of these items get lost or destroyed as time moves on and an increasing number of people have the desire to collect such pieces of history – the result inevitably tends to be an excess demand over supply.

Leaving you with these initial thoughts we now approach Part 1 and the background to scripophily.

PART 1

General background and history

THE DEVELOPMENT OF SCRIPOPHILY

Scripophily, the collecting of old bonds and share certificates, began in earnest following the publication of two catalogues in Germany listing and illustrating most of the bonds issued by pre-revolutionary China and Russia – the latter covering railroads only. The catalogues were the result of doctoral research by two German bankers, Ulrich Drumm and Alfons Henseler. They were first published in 1976, but it was a further two years before a major commercial development took place with the entrée of stamp dealers, Stanley Gibbons.

Gibbons began by issuing monthly price lists, and in 1978 started a series of public auctions. Coming at a peak inflationary period when people were seeking alternatives to money and the more usual investment fields, the result was startling. Fuelled by bullish press articles and constantly rising list prices, investors poured in surplus cash and retail prices of Chinese bonds rose a staggering 1,500 per cent over seventeen months. Russian railway bonds fared more modestly, with only a 640 per cent increase! Although these figures are based on retail prices, investors were still able to make remarkable profits in a matter of months, often achieving them before being billed for their original purchase. This feat was facilitated by the continuing stock market quote of most Chinese and Russian bonds. There thus developed a most unusual feature – the 'double market', of which more later.

The pace continued unabated for almost two years during which time a record price of £14,000 was paid for a Chinese £500 bond of 1898 (German issue) at auction and the price of the 5% Chinese Government loan of 1908 reached 1,000 per cent (of face value) on the London Stock Exchange. Auction houses saw their opportunities and soon Sotheby, Christies and Phillips were holding regular auctions in London supplemented by many other houses in Germany, Holland, New York and Switzerland.

The inevitable crash happened between November 1979 and April 1980.

Before looking at the reasons for the fall, let us first examine the reasons for the rise. There were six major factors which caused or encouraged the emergence of scripophily as an investment medium:

1 Availability of basic catalogues and publication of frequently increasing prices lists.
2 An inflationary period with faith lost in holding cash.
3 Continuing stock market activity in Chinese and Russian bonds (the 'double market').
4 Other 'alternative investments', such as stamps, already at very high levels.
5 Known rarity of the products.
6 Their intrinsic attractive, unusual and historical features.

Of these factors, the availability of catalogues together with the bonds' rarity, attractiveness and historical interest, were fundamentally sound reasons for the establishment of a new collecting field, and it is these factors to which we will return in Part 3 on developing a collection.

STOCK MARKET INFLUENCE

Mention was made earlier of the 'double market' phenomenon of prices being determined by both dealers and the stock market. This also appears as an important contributing factor to the rise of scripophily and because the feature is unique to this collecting field it is worth elaborating on the subject.

Almost all bonds collected today were, at one time or another, quoted on a stock market, whether London, Paris, New York or elsewhere. In the normal course of their life they would have been redeemed and cancelled in accordance with the terms of the loan. Some, such as US Railroad bonds may have been absorbed by other companies through takeover or merger before the end of their intended life, but others

£100 bond of Imperial China issued in 1908. These were actively traded on the London Stock Market reaching one thousand per cent (£1,000) at the peak of speculation in 1979.

were defaulted. A default occurs when the borrower (government or company) fails to meet interest payments and ceases bond redemption. The act of default does not result in the removal of a stock exchange quotation as it is always hoped that the position will be corrected in the future. Several countries or states, legal or otherwise, defaulted on their bonds, thus creating the basic scrip of scripophily. Major defaults are summarized in the table below.

MAJOR INTERNATIONAL DEFAULTS

Country/State	Approximate amount defaulted (principal only)
China	£60,000,000
Russia	£1,000,000,000 plus
Confederate States of America	$712,000,000
Mexico	$12,000,000
State of Mississippi	$7,000,000

Not all the above remain in default. Certain countries, particularly those of South America have, over recent years, almost wholly cleared their debts. Although Confederate bonds remain unpaid the stock market quote has been dropped, but this did not happen until the 1890s. The two main defaulters are China and Russia and it was the bonds of these two nations which fuelled the price rises.

For years prices of Chinese and Russian bonds hovered around 1–5% of face value, but with the advent of the collector market stockbrokers and jobbers saw an excellent opportunity to dispose of large dormant holdings. Unfortunately, many of the individual bond issues were relatively small and it was not difficult for those well versed in stock market practice to cause dramatic price movements, pushing up the prices of certain bonds to unrealistic levels and these high prices subsequently became the dealers' cost of purchase.

No other collecting field could boast a secondary market of such sophistication, but in the final analysis it was the activities of that very market which were chiefly responsible for the volatile price fluctuations in the early days of scripophily. Many fingers were burnt in the City and it is unlikely that the stock market will be used again as a touchstone for price explosion.

REASONS FOR THE FALL

Since itemizing the various 'reasons for the rise', we have been slightly diverted by the stock market issue, but as this was a major cause of the fall, it was, perhaps, opportune. Other factors were:

1 Little effort was made by dealers to develop the collector base. All attention was concentrated on the investor.
2 Fast price rises attracted the short-term speculator, who knew nothing of the subject, but was only interested in financial gain. After 12–18 months their objective was to realize paper profits – unfortunately, all acted in unison.
3 Prices moved too fast to allow potential collectors to enter the field for a modest outlay.
4 A lack of follow-up publications, particularly reference and introductory books, and magazines. The original catalogues were unfortunately in German and rapidly went out of print.
5 Too many auctions took place in relation to the number of collectors.
6 The beginning of economic recession and a fall in the rate of inflation.

A sharp rise followed by a dramatic fall is not an uncommon feature in the early life of a new collecting hobby, and scripophily has emerged from its birth pains stronger and healthier for the experience. Events since the fall are evidence of this and we continue with a summary of the major features.

LATER PROGRESS

Since April 1980, and despite the departure of many of the original investors, the number of collectors has grown considerably in all parts of the world. This growth continues but has a long way to go to catch up with an estimated 15–20 million stamp collectors or the many millions of banknote, coin, map and medal collectors. It is this enormous potential growth which many new collectors find so fascinating. From an initial base of around 300 collectors, estimates now put the figure at 25–30,000. This increase has been achieved over four to five years and has been accompanied and encouraged by the establishment of many new dealers and local collectors' societies throughout the world stretching from New York to Australia. A list of major dealers and societies is given on page 139.

The number of publications, both reference material and magazines, has also increased and this book bears testament to that development. A number are listed in the appendix for your information. But, perhaps of all the reasons for the growth, the most important has been the broadening of the field. No longer do Chinese and Russian bonds dominate the market. The establishment of the hobby in the wide range of countries has naturally led to the growth of local preferences; thus Swiss material has great demand in Switzerland, early German shares in Germany, Palestine material amongst the Jewish community, Australian shares in Australia, and so on.

But apart from these localized biases, certain other sectors have risen to rank with China and Russia as *internationally* acceptable. The most notable of these is US Railroads. A vast field covering over 9,000 different companies and a time span of over one hundred years, both share certificates and bonds are extremely attractive, often with vignettes of early trains and station scenes. The railroads were a major feature in the early history of the United States and, consequently, it is not suprising that it is this sector which has become most popular in America itself. Collectors from all countries, however, have also chosen this as their field of specialization.

And so, as research goes on, scripophily develops. Still at an early stage in its life cycle, collectors can look forward to exciting advances over the coming years.

WHAT ARE BONDS AND SHARES?

To many of us the thought of financial mechanics with $ and % signs causes the same initial effect as algebra – a mental blackout. This section sets out to ease the way and cut through some of the inevitable jargon, which, more than anything else, is chiefly responsible for the 'fear of finance'.

THE DIFFERENCE BETWEEN THE TWO

Collecting bonds and shares necessarily requires a basic knowledge of finance, but the depth of that knowledge is very much up to the individual scripophilist. As a minimum, this is all you need to know: apart from trading profits, a company of whatever size, obtains its finances from two main sources namely, shareholders (the owners of the company) and lenders. The latter may be banks, governments or private individuals, who provide funds for a limited period at an agreed rate of interest. If things go badly for the company, the lenders still get paid, but the shareholders may well not as they have no guaranteed return on their investment. Conversely, of course, when the company is successful and business is booming the shareholders stand to benefit most as they have taken the greater risk and will reap the larger returns accordingly. Loans to a company take several forms, the most common of which is the bank overdraft, another is through the issue of bonds.

So there we have it, share certificates are evidence of an individual's investment in the ownership of a company, and bonds are evidence of an individual's loan to a company.

The financially faint-hearted may like to stop at this juncture and move to the next chapter but for the benefit of the determined, a little more detail follows.

It is important to remember that although the bonds and shares collected today were usually issued many years ago, the mechanics of issuing such documents remains little changed. The earliest companies were formed by entrepreneurs contributing capital and personal involvement. It was not until the mid-seventeenth century that the idea of diversification of investment through participation in several companies rather than a single outlet, became fashionable. Thus, in a London coffee house the stock exchange process began. Shares were bought and sold at market prices and ownership changes were recorded on the certificates themselves. And so we come to a most important classification: Registered and Bearer and the collector of scrip must be aware of the distinction between the two.

REGISTERED v. BEARER

Early certificates, whether shares, bonds or other loan documents were mostly issued 'To Bearer'. This meant that the investment in the company could be sold or passed on to a new individual without reference to the company concerned. Physical possession of the bond – assuming it wasn't stolen or obtained by fraudulent means – was all important. This system kept records to a minimum and put the onus of dividend or interest distribution on the investor rather than the company, which, of course, was unaware of the names and addresses of its financiers. So far as investors were concerned a notable benefit was the consequent secrecy; no one, not even the tax-collector, could ascertain the investments of a particular individual from a company's records.

This emphasis on bearer share certificates continued for many years and in some countries, such as Switzerland, is still the norm. Many governments, however, felt the need to tighten up on controls and imposed a requirement for share registration, thus ensuring the jobs of large hordes of company registrars!

By now, you will probably have realized the significance of registered versus bearer to the collector. As a bearer share is not issued to anyone in particular it does not have to be cancelled and re-issued when sold, thus the number of bearer shares is limited to the authorized capital of the company; an amount usually printed on the certificates. On the other hand, a registered share must be re-registered whenever sold, and the original cancelled or destroyed. As there is no limit to the number of times a share may change hands, there is similarly no limit to the number of certificates which may now exist.

Attention has so far been concentrated on shares, but we now turn to bonds. Almost all bonds are 'bearer'. They are usually issued by a company or government internationally and may be held by anyone, anywhere in the world (exchange controls permitting); for this reason it is important to minimize paperwork. Considerable detail is printed on the document itself giving the investor exact instructions for obtaining interest and eventual repayment of principal. Occasionally, as with the Chinese for example, instructions are printed in several languages. During their life, on which subject more detail later, they change hands frequently, and if lost, a duplicate may be issued, but clearly identified as such. Thus, the number of bonds issued by a particular borrower is known exactly, and because such information is of interest to the investor, it is almost always printed on the bond itself.

REPAYMENT

The terms 'issued', 'redeemed' and 'outstanding' require some explanation. Reference has already been made to the relatively unchanged mechanics governing the issue and repayment of bonds over the years. Bonds were not only issued in the past to build the early railroads of the Americas or finance Imperial China's balance of payments, they continue to be issued today by governments and companies in even greater numbers – albeit not so decoratively. Whatever technical jargon is used to describe them (euro-bonds, $ straights, Bulldogs, etc.) they are still bonds in the original form but with minor variations. Their beginning and end is summarized as follows:

Issue	Detailed information on the borrower is prepared and a group of underwriters (usually banks) is assembled. A few of this group are selected as the issuing banks, often covering several countries. The bond is launched into the market to be branded 'triple A' or whatever rating the investment community deems appropriate.
Redeemed and Outstanding	Bonds are a debt, and as such must be repaid over a specified number of years, not simply at the end of the borrowing term. This is an important feature and you will understand the process better by studying the small print on a particular bond. All state the period of the loan and also indicate from which year repayment begins, so that by the end of the total period, all bonds have been fully redeemed. Thus, after the grace period, there will always be some bonds which are 'outstanding' and some which have been repaid. As time passes, the former become less.

It is the calculation of the number of bonds redeemed which can cause most problems for the scripophilist seeking to ascertain rarity.

There are two alternative methods adopted by borrowers for redemption of bonds. The simplest (albeit least common) is that chosen by the Chinese. In this case a constant percentage of bonds was repaid each year; thus, if the loan was for a period of fifty years and twenty-five years elapsed before default, then it is correct to assume that fifty per cent of the original bonds should have been repaid.

The more usual procedure, however, complicates the calculation. In this case, the total monetary value of the loan including interest is divided by the number of repaying years. The resulting figure represents the amount of money which the borrower must put aside annually in order to meet interest payments and gradually redeem the bonds (known as the 'sinking fund'). Unfortunately, this is not as simple as it sounds, for in early years most of the sinking fund goes towards interest and very few bonds are redeemed (similar to a British building society mortgage); as time passes, however, an increasing amount of the principal is repaid but it is a complex calculation to work out the exact number of redemptions at a specific time.

In view of the many potential pitfalls in attempting to accurately determine the number of outstanding bonds of a particular issue, collectors should seek out the detailed stock market records.

One final point on redemption relates to the choice of which bonds are selected for payment. This is often determined by lot and the serial numbers of those bonds to be redeemed are published in the press.

DEBENTURES

Before leaving the financial background, mention should also be made of the 'debenture' – a document which many collectors will come across, similar in form and function to a bond but slightly different within the company law framework. Always of a limited issue to cover a specific borrowing need, the debenture, for tax reasons, proved most popular with British companies. Although often of low issue, their design is usually less elaborate than a bond, although of a similar size.

PRINTING AND ENGRAVING

Some time has already been spent explaining the difference between 'bearer' and 'registered' certificates, from which the reader will appreciate the dangers of forgery in the case of the former. It was primarily for this reason that companies or governments issuing bearer stock went to great lengths and expense to deter the prospective forger.

TECHNIQUES

As with banknotes, the most effective deterrent was a combination of high quality paper, skilled engraving and intricate design. The same companies who printed banknotes and postage stamps were employed as producers of bonds and share certificates. Early engraving techniques involved cutting into a copper or steel plate with the use of tools such as a burin or graver. Skilled engravers knew how deep to cut the plate in order to create different depths of design and perspective. Up to the early nineteenth century copper plates were used which, being softer than the steel plates commonly employed thereafter, had a limited life.

The four names appearing most frequently as printers of certificates are Waterlow & Sons, Bradbury Wilkinson and De La Rue of England and the American Bank Note Company of the United States. From 1858, the latter incorporated seven other American printing companies and in 1879 took Bradbury Wilkinson under its wing, followed by the Canadian Bank Note Company in 1911.

The security printing department of each firm held a number of engravers trained for specific tasks. Highest status was afforded the engraver of portraits, as this entailed the greatest amount of skill and experience. There would be another who specialized in vignettes – landscapes, buildings, trains, groups of people, etc., and a third who was the letter engraver entrusted with transmitting the name of the company or country, text, and other details.

Some time in the early nineteenth century the American, Jacob Perkins (who later settled in England and formed Perkins Bacon, Crown Agents) invented the transference method of security printing. This allowed for relatively fast production of large numbers of certificates while still maintaining the individuality necessary to prevent easy forgery. Each engraver worked on a separate plate, using up only the area allotted for his specialized task. The engravings on each plate were then transferred to a master plate.

Colours were applied by means of separate plates or by use of the lithographic method whereby a 'stone' is waxed and the areas which will later take the ink are scraped away. Another mechanical process was instrumental in the engraving techniques found on bonds and shares from about the mid-nineteenth century and helped to make forgery difficult, if not impossible. Asa Spencer, a founder of the American Bank Note Company, invented the geometrical lathe for making ornamental borders. By means of discs and gear wheels which moved together, a series of complex patterns were formed by a diamond-tipped point moving over a plate. An infinite variety of settings – and hence patterns – was possible.

DESIGNING

Companies or countries normally suggested their own designs, which is why Chinese and Russian bonds and shares look distinctly Chinese or Russian despite the fact that some of the Russian and probably all of the Chinese were designed and printed by western firms. The art departments of security printing firms produced designs for the approval of the client – as well as lettering, these often contained vignettes related to the country, town or organization issuing the certificates. After approval of the design, the artist composed a detailed watercolour to be copied by engravers. Certificates engraved by American printing firms, in particular from the nineteenth century onwards, are characterized by the liberal use of cherubs and pseudo-Grecian mythological figures intermingling with trains and other signs of modern industry.

It is often interesting to compare designs and a self-trained eye can soon begin to spot common features. These features may be the result of a government, such as Russia, wanting to preserve an image of consistency or, as is more usual, a printer using existing designs in new formats. For example, many of the trains appearing on US railroad certificates reappear on both Chinese and Russian banknotes.

The use of existing part plates naturally reduced the cost of printing but another alternative was also employed for the production of registered share certificates. Not being bearer (and thus less open to forgery), these could be 'neatly lithographed or printed letterpress, without incurring the cost of engraving a specially designed plate . . .' as advertised by Waterlow in their General Catalogue of 1912.

However, not all bearer material was as carefully prepared as suggested here. There are cases, and the bonds issued by the US Confederacy are prime examples, where scant attention was paid to the dangers of forgery. Out of the 170 or so different bond types, only four were carefully engraved. Those four are the Tri-value Cotton Bonds of 1863 which were clearly engraved in Europe but it is not known by whom. Other Confederate bonds were printed on poor quality paper, which accounts for their often poor condition today. Ten different printing houses were used to produce the certificates in Charleston, Columbia, Richmond and New Orleans.

FUTURE DEVELOPMENTS

Despite the engravers' efforts there have been occasions, especially in recent years, when the temptation to forge has been too great. Only those cases discovered are known, but those have been sufficient to encourage at least one august body – the United States Treasury – to do away with physical bonds and replace them with computer print-outs. Not only a sign of the times, but a further indication of the increasing historical significance of the scrip of the past.

HISTORY AND ART IN SCRIPOPHILY

History and art are as much a part of scripophily as economics. The raising of money is often a function of historical development, and in the last two hundred years it might be argued that without money, 'history' might not have happened, or at least happened very differently.

The industrial revolution which began in England around the 1780s with the building of the Iron Bridge at Coalbrookdale, is the most important historical event reflected in bonds and shares. The growth of the iron and steel industry and, more particularly, the birth and development of the railways, set the scene throughout the world for the establishment of numerous companies' and government construction projects, all of which needed financing by loans or shareholders' funds.

The novelty of industry was portrayed on many early certificates with views of multi-chimneyed factories vigorously polluting the atmosphere for the good of mankind. Such evidence of manufacture was reassuring to prospective shareholders and, for many, a picture of the establishment on a share certificate was the nearest they actually came to seeing their investments. Thus, factories, railway bridges and mine workings were favourite decorations on early share certificates. For certain companies, these signs of property and activity were very much limited to the certificates themselves, and on more than one occasion investors were encouraged to part with their money through fanciful views of company activity.

THE SOUTH SEA BUBBLE

Mention has already been made of the industrial revolution and its impact on the number of companies established and the format of their share certificates; but it was over fifty years prior to this period that company finance really got under way.

The South Sea Company, founded by Robert Harley in 1711, was perhaps the most celebrated and earliest of corporate disasters. Formed to trade with Spanish America, investors were persuaded to exchange State annuities for South Sea stock priced at a hefty premium. The company took over the whole of the National Debt, and its stock, with a guaranteed 6% interest rate, rocketed from a price of $128\frac{1}{2}$ in January of 1720 to 1,000 in July of the same year. In September the 'bubble burst' and the price collapsed to 175. Share certificates do not appear to have existed as it is believed that shareholders' names were entered in a register and only a receipt handed to the unfortunate victim. Receipts reappear from time to time, and although plain looking, are fascinating reminders of this most famous bankruptcy.

BETSY ROSS AND THE FLAG

A rather more positive piece of history recorded on a certificate was the birth of the Stars and Stripes. Betsy Ross is famous in American history for creating the flag following the revolution. In 1899, the 'American Flag House and Betsy Ross Memorial Association' was formed and the public invited to subscribe. The certificates which were issued are extremely attractive depicting the sewing Betsy with her husband, George Washington and Robert Morris looking on in undisguised admiration.

THE STAR OF TEXAS

Following the eventual defeat of the Spaniards in Texas in 1836, a republic was founded led by such figures as Stephen F. Austin. The Texans' original objective was to join the United States but it was not until 1845 that this was achieved, during which time the State operated as an independent country. Nowhere is this more clearly highlighted than in the bonds issued to finance its development. Many were signed by Austin and bear the famous 'lone star' symbol. Several issues were denominated in £ sterling as well as US $ indicating the close economic links with Britain which were encouraged by the State as a means of pressurizing the United States.

THE AMERICAN CIVIL WAR

The first shot was fired on 12 April 1861, when Southern troops under the command of General P. G. T. Beauregard, one of the most flamboyant characters of the war and whose picture featured on two Confederate bond issues, launched their 40-hour bombardment of Fort Sumpter, Charleston. But it was not until 21 July that the two armies met for the first major battle – Bull Run.

Bull Run was a disaster for the North and their performance over the next two years was little improved. Major reasons were lack of military leadership and an unfounded overconfidence at the outset. Both sides felt the war would be short-lived and neither called up troops in sufficient numbers. The North frequently enrolled men for 90 day stints, and pay was invariably late. Some Northern (Union) bond issues were used solely to fund the troops' wages; for example, State of New York 7% loan, 'Repayment of Bounties to Volunteers'. But despite the ingenuity and military skill of the Confederate General, Robert E. Lee, the North's superior resources of men and material eventually triumphed on 9 April 1865 when Lee was

A Confederate Cotton Bond of 1863 – denominated in £ sterling, French Francs and bales of cotton. A fine example of engraved Confederate material.

surrounded and forced to surrender by General Ulysses S. Grant at Appomatox Court House. Within one month the war was ended.

The lack of financial independence of the Confederacy resulted in the need to raise large foreign loans. The endless demand for cotton, in Britain and France in particular, made the raising of such loans feasible as many were guaranteed against cotton bails. Some, such as the 1863 loan of £3 million, were even denominated in cotton. The bails set aside for these loans were ultimately destroyed by the victors. The amount of money borrowed and eventually defaulted by the Confederate States was enormous, with one issue alone exceeding $147 million.

The history of the occasion is further emphasized by the portraits displayed on the bonds themselves. Most Confederate leaders are depicted on one or more issues. As well as such notables as General 'Stonewall' Jackson and President Jefferson Davis, the whole political cabinet got coverage (bond numbers refer to the Criswell catalogue; see bibliography).

NAME	POSITION	BONDS ON WHICH THEY APPEAR
Jefferson Davis	President	4, 85, 86, 95, 125
Alexander Stephens	Vice-President	70, 123
Robert Toombs (Georgia)	Secretary of State	37
Christopher Memminger (S.Carolina)	Secretary of the Treasury	59, 84, 87, 88, 92, 97, 98, 102, 110, 111, 124
L. P. Walker (Alabama)	Secretary of War	21
Stephen R. Mallory (Florida)	Secretary of the Navy	33, 34, 40, 63, 67, 89
John H. Reagan (Texas)	Postmaster General	36, 62, 101
J. P. Benjamin (Louisiana)	Attorney General	31, 43, 57, 60, 61, 65, 71, 75, 100

£50 bond in the Shanghai-Hangchow Ningpo Railway of 1936. The portrait of Sun Yat-sen commemorates twenty-five years after the Revolution.

Opposite above: A most unusual example of the American Flag House and Betsy Ross Memorial Association certificate. Issued in 1899.

Opposite below: A bearer share in the Jewish Colonial Trust Ltd, c. 1900.

Later cabinet reshuffles resulted in J. P. Benjamin becoming Secretary of State and George W. Randolph Secretary of War (bonds 42, 64, 68). Not only were Confederate celebrities portrayed, but also the famous founders of America. George Washington figured prominently on many issues, and even Benjamin Franklin and John C. Calhoun made their appearance – the objective being to convince foreign investors of the legality of their cause.

PALESTINE

Well across the other side of the Atlantic and over thirty years later, another cause was beginning to surface and be reflected by an interesting issue of shares.

The Jewish Colonial Trust formed in 1899 represented the aspirations of the Zionist movement led by Dr Theodor Herzl towards establishment of a Jewish state. It was intended to be the financial arm – a sort

American Flag House and Betsy Ross Memorial Association

CERTIFICATE Nº C   ISSUE 1899.

This is to Certify that _____ of _____ is a member of the AMERICAN FLAG HOUSE AND BETSY ROSS MEMORIAL ASSOCIATION and a Subscriber to the fund for the purchase and preservation of the HISTORIC HOUSE in which the FIRST FLAG OF THE UNITED STATES OF AMERICA was manufactured for the erection of a NATIONAL MEMORIAL in honor of BETSY ROSS. The names of all Subscribers are placed on the ROLL OF HONOR and preserved in the ARCHIVES OF THE ASSOCIATION

Edward Brooks
PRESIDENT

Adam H. Fetterolf
VICE PRESIDENT

John Quincy Adams
SECRETARY

Geo Clinton Batcheller
TREASURER

THE
JEWISH COLONIAL TRUST
(JUEDISCHE COLONIALBANK)
LIMITED.
CAPITAL £2,000,000.

ORDINARY SHARE CERTIFICATE   £1 Ordinary Shares

DIVIDED INTO
1,000,000 ORDINARY SHARES OF £1 EACH & 100 FOUNDERS SHARES OF £1 EACH
THE FIRST ADMINISTRATION OF 1899 (5659).

Nº 376

Coupons 7-36 issued

This is to Certify that Simon Treisman Esqr of 24 Hunt Street Brick Lane London England is the Registered Holder of One Ordinary Shares numbered 001698 to _____ inclusive in The Jewish Colonial Trust Juedische Colonialbank Limited, subject to the Memorandum and Articles of Association thereof and that the sum of ONE POUND has been paid up on each of the said Shares.

GIVEN under the Common Seal of the said Company this 13th day of February 1900

17

of Jewish East India company – to gather money for building industries, railways and the buying of land in Palestine. The Jewish Colonial Trust, chartered in London, arose out of the first and second Zionist Congresses in Basel which decided to create an independent financial institution '. . . to develop colonization, the natural resources, industries of the country and to create working opportunities'.

By 1956 there were over 100,000 shareholders; however, the institution seems to have been more enthusiastically received among the poor than the rich and this may be one reason for its failure to achieve its original aims. Even an early supporter of the Trust, a Dr Gaster, speaking at a rally admitted that they were merely building the first rung of the ladder. Did anyone imagine that the whole of Palestine could be bought for £2 million he asked rhetorically? 'Not for £100 million could one buy that land.' He said that he would welcome the rich and that they were wrong to work against the Trust. It had been called a trust, he said, because the money of the Jewish nations in Europe would be kept in trust for the Jewish nation in Palestine.

The Trust may not have been the main instrument in the formation of the Jewish State as it wished, but it did at least have one major achievement. It created a Jewish bank, its present-day successor being Bank Leumi.

The original share certificates list the directors headed by David Wolffsohn and the four vignettes represent industry, trade, agriculture and faith.

It would be easy to continue indefinitely describing historical events depicted or reflected in bonds and shares. Many will occur in other parts of this book but to be totally comprehensive would require several additional volumes. Historical references must therefore draw to a close, but not without brief mention of just one of many tales from China.

CHINA

The Shanghai-Hangchow-Ningpo Railway was begun in 1907 and the 1936 6% bonds were issued to finance completion of the project with the building of a bridge across the Chien Tang. The face of the bonds carries a portrait of Sun Yat-sen and the back bears a fine picture of the bridge which was completed in 1937, only seven days before being blown up by the Chinese Army as it retreated from the Japanese advance. Thus 1937 is a significant date for scripophilists as it set the scene for the Chinese default, without which scripophily might never have hit the headlines.

ART FOR MONEY'S SAKE

Much has already been said about the printing and engraving of bonds and shares and reference already made to the involvement of artists in their design. Just as industrial scenes or portraits of serious gentlemen played their part in persuading investors to invest, so too did art.

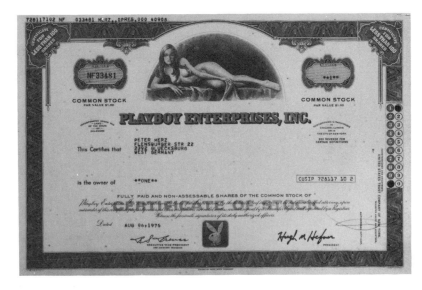

Playboy Enterprises Inc.

Opposite: *One of the last Chinese bond issues under the Emperor – the Hukuang Railway bond of 1911.*

It was, of course, inevitable that the artistic style of a period was reflected in the design of certificates of that period, but this was not the case for all countries. British certificates, for example, have been consistently plain with few frills. US Railroads have concentrated on depicting trains or station scenes at the expense of elaborate designs. But others, particularly French certificates of the 1920s are of clear 'art nouveau' derivation and some, such as that of 'Paris France', actually designed by Alphonse Mucha himself. Most French material is extremely ornate as are also many of the Spanish shares.

But art takes many forms, and precise design work can be as pleasing as the most elaborate images – both have the advantage of making the forger's task that much more difficult. The portrayal of a naked lady on a recent Playboy Enterprises share certificate can hardly be considered a cultural contribution, but it nevertheless displays the company's 'product' as succinctly as a smoking chimney describes an active factory!

PART 2

Collecting themes

INTRODUCTION

A brief glance at the contents page will already have alerted the reader to the fact that this section on collecting themes constitutes the greater part of the book. Despite its length, it certainly does not profess to be fully comprehensive, and there are many subjects only briefly referred to and some not mentioned at all. The objective, nevertheless, is to present to the prospective collector a number of themes together with some background to each, which may help determine the subject to be followed.

Choosing a collecting theme at the outset is a difficult, albeit enjoyable, task. Some may wish to defer the decision by first purchasing a selection of material, such as the 'starter packs' provided by most dealers, this approach is fine and gives the collector a personal feel of the alternatives; others may prefer to go directly to their chosen field. Whichever approach is chosen, it is important to pick a theme and concentrate on collecting rather than simply accumulating.

Part 2 has been divided into two sections, the first by country and the second by subject. Such a division implies a degree of exclusivity which is unfortunate as both subjects and countries inevitably overlap.

Considerable attention has been paid to the historical background to the themes and it is hoped that this will demonstrate the enormously significant part reflected by bonds and shares in the socio-economic development of the world. The comments and anecdotes are intended to encourage further research and not to represent a comprehensive history. Remember, this is only the tip of the iceberg and you, the collector, must carry on the exploration.

AUSTRALIA

Being a relatively young country with a small population, Australia may be thought to have little to offer the scripophilist. This is certainly not the case for, despite these factors, the country, because of its size, distance from the West and huge mineral resources, makes an ideal collecting theme with material mirroring its economic and social development.

The collector should be warned at the outset, however, that despite the many companies formed both in Australia and in Europe to finance Australian trade, the amount of known pre-1900 material is very limited.

EARLY HISTORY

Twenty-seven years elapsed after the settlement landing at Sydney Cove in 1788, before the first out-of-town road was constructed. In 1802, the population was no more than 6,000 persons and 8,632 sheep, but it was the latter, with the assistance of the breeding techniques of a certain John Macarthur, which were primarily responsible for the country's early growth.

Until this period most of the high-quality wool needed for Britain's mills had come from Saxony. For strategic reasons the country wished to reduce this dependence on Europe and the availability of large amounts of top-quality wool from Australia fitted the bill perfectly. By 1830, as much as 2 million pounds weight a year was being exported to Britain.

The early years to 1850 were centred around the pastoral development of the country and as farming expanded, so the major towns were founded: Brisbane in 1824, Perth in 1829, Adelaide in 1836 and Melbourne in 1835. But it was in 1851 when the real fireworks started.

GOLD AND MINERALS

Mention is later made in this book of the great gold rushes of the 1850s. Australia played a major part with discoveries being made in Victoria, New South Wales and Queensland. Everything suddenly revolved around gold and, as in California, the need was for transport – at any cost. Australia got its 'American Express' in the form of Cobb & Co., formed and run extremely successfully by four young Americans, one of whom (John M. Peck) had served his apprenticeship in America with Wells Fargo and Co. As in the United States, express business proved extremely profitable and Freeman Cobb, an extremely capable expressman.

Rough terrain and widely spread townships ideally suited the American built coaches, and the use of horse-drawn vehicles continued well into the twentieth century. The introduction of the steam railway in many ways complemented the coaches, which were able to operate from ever new station bases. The first railway was built by the Melbourne and Hobson's Bay Railway Co. in 1854 and ran from Melbourne to Sandridge (now Port Melbourne), a distance of two miles. As more mineral discoveries were made, copper in the mid-1870s at Cobar, tin in Tasmania in 1871 and silver in the 1880s, so the railways expanded. Between 1875 and 1891 mileage rose from 1,600 miles to 10,000 miles and as well as serving the coastline they stretched well inland.

Cobb & Co. was acquired by James Rutherford who ran it for fifty years. Together with Dan Williams he formed the first iron works in Australia in 1874 – the Eskbank Iron Co. and in 1881 incorporated Cobb & Co. with a nominal capital of £50,000 composed of 500 £100 shares, of which 300 were issued. Should such certificates still exist today, they would be of tremendous interest to the collectors of Australian material.

Mineral discoveries continued (and indeed still continue) throughout the latter part of the century and in 1883 Charles Rasp first discovered the varied riches of Broken Hill – a venture eventually resulting in the country's largest private enterprise – the Broken Hill Pty Company. The opening of the goldfields of Kalgoorlie and Coolgardie in the early 1890s renewed the enthusiasm for gold but it was the growth of secondary industries which caused a marked shift in population from the country to the towns, eventually making Sydney and Melbourne two of the world's largest cities. The growth of railways continued, reaching a peak of 27,000 miles of track in 1941 but, despite encouragement to standardize, several different gauges were used and full compatability was not achieved until 1970.

Above: *The Panama, New Zealand & Australian Royal Mail Co. Ltd, an early certificate of 1867.*

Left: *One of the earliest Australian share certificates in the Bank of Australia.*

CERTIFICATES AND COLLECTORS

As previously indicated there appears to be relatively little Australian scrip around and building up a collection can be difficult. There is no doubt that material exists and the collector choosing this theme is advised to concentrate on the following sectors:

Banks (probably the earliest being around 1825)
Railways (from 1854)
Gold Mining – two periods: 1851–60 and1890–1900
Tasmania

The possibility of compiling a collection closely related to the growth of a country is a real one in the case of Australia and should prove an exciting challenge.

CHINA

As one of the first sectors of scripophily to be researched, many current collectors find themselves with a fair smattering of these bonds and many wonder why. It is perhaps an understatement to say that Chinese material rose to fame on a catalogue, Chinese bonds *became the market.* Between March 1978 and November 1979, their prices rose monthly, and on certain occasions, daily. Press comment concentrated on the issues and collectors and investors poured money into them at a rate which would have made Sun Yat-sen proud.

Apart from the issue of a catalogue, there were other reasons which made Chinese bonds the speculators' target – many perfectly sound reasons, but not over such a short time frame. The bonds themselves are extremely finely engraved, they are of generally low issue and are 'exotic' therefore, international. But more significantly they retained a stock market quotation the impact of which has already been discussed at length in Part 1.

Rather than concentrate on the investment appeal of Chinese bonds, this chapter will be devoting more attention to the history behind them. Chinese history is extremely complex consisting of numerous civil wars, political conflicts, foreign interventions and unpronounceable names. What follows is a considerably simplified version of the period which concerns scripophilists, namely 1898–1938, during which time most international bond issues occurred. There is a surprisingly close relationship between historical development and the bonds themselves and this aspect will be emphasized.

THE NINETEENTH CENTURY

Throughout the nineteenth century the major powers – Britain, Russia and France – sought permanent bases in China. Whereas Russia was keen to establish an eastern seaboard (and possibly the eventual surrounding of the country), Britain, France and later Germany, were intent on preserving the profitable trading outposts based largely on tea, silk and opium. Several land licences were granted, the main ones being Hong Kong to the British, Amur province as far south as Vladivostock to the Russians, and Indo-China (now Vietnam) to France.

Although in later years, the continued presence of foreign governments led to major uprisings, in the mid-nineteenth century there were considerable benefits to the country particularly with regard to industrialization and the development of its infrastructure. The 1870s saw the beginnings of industrial revolution and several government-supervised companies were established; amongst these were the following:

The China Merchants Steam Navigation Co. (1872)
Shanghai Cotton Cloth Mill (1878)
Imperial Telegraph Administration (1881)

A naval academy was established at Tientsin in 1880 but perhaps, most significant of all, the first steam railway was opened in 1876.

The early development of railways is dealt with at some length in the chapter on Railways but it is interesting to note the political significance of railways and their impact on certain major events in Chinese history. The Russians, for example, sought to pressurize the country by building the Trans-Siberia Railway as close to the northern borders of China as possible with a view to annexing Mongolia, Manchuria and Korea. At a later date (1911) the revolution led by Sun Yat-sen to oust the Manchu government was sparked off by a government decision to take over all the country's main railways. In view of their significance both to history and to bonds we will return to railways shortly with a typical example of the building and financing process.

In 1894 Japan declared war on China and by the following year had inflicted considerable defeats, gaining Formosa (now Taiwan), the Liao-tung peninsula, and also obtaining independence for Korea. Fears of Japan becoming too powerful caused the major powers to put pressure on the victor to moderate its demands, and as a reward for Russia's assistance in regaining the Liao-tung peninsula, it was granted authority to build the Chinese Eastern Railway right across Manchuria to Vladivostock, thus completing the Trans-Siberia Line.

The seemingly endless land-grabbing by outside governments resulted in the formation of a nationalist society popularly known as the Boxers, although more correctly 'The Society of Righteous Harmonious

*£20 bond of the 1913
Reorganisation Loan – total
funds of £25,000,000 were used
to quell disturbances.*

Fists'. The result of their uprising, culminating in the siege of foreign embassies in Peking in 1900, had the opposite effect to their objective. Foreign governments put down the revolt with an international force and resumed intervention in a rather more determined fashion.

1900–38

Continuing dissatisfaction with the Manchu government's failure to curb foreign land-grabbing led to the formation of a major new revolutionary movement. Its leader was Dr Sun Yat-sen. By 1911 revolution had spread across the land and in February 1912 the last Emperor of China abdicated, making way for the Republic. This change of government is most clearly highlighted in the wording on the bonds themselves, which, prior to 1912 were issued 'by Imperial Edict' (as on the Hukuang Railway bonds of 1911, for example) but thereafter carried the words 'created by virtue of a resolution of the National Assembly of Peking'. One of the first issues to be so described was that of the Lung-Tsing-U-Hai Railway 1913 loan.

Sun Yat-sen did not have control of the military forces, however, and was forced to resign the presidency of the Republic in 1912. He moved to the south and formed the Nationalist Party (the Kuomintang). But the uprising was put down by the Government which had anticipated civil war and under Yuan Shih-K'ai persuaded the five major powers of Britain, France, Germany, Japan and Russia to pull together a

One of the builders of Chinese railways – the Cie Générale de Chemins de Fer et de Tramways en Chine.

£25 million foreign loan to finance military preparations. The issue was known as the 1913 Chinese Government Reorganization Loan. The bonds are some of the finest engraved of all Chinese items and many have found their way into frames decorating offices and homes.

Sun Yat-sen fled the country coming under the powerful influence of the Bolsheviks, who sought to gain control of China through the Kuomintang. Sun Yat-sen died in 1925, but his portrait appears on several bond issues after that date, the most important being the 1934 Indemnity Loan and the 6% Shanghai-Hangchow-Ningpo Railway Loan of 1936.

The new leader of the Kuomintang was Chiang Kai-shek, who had spent the previous two years in training in the Soviet Union. Early military successes encouraged him to take a more adventurous line against the advice of his Russian advisers; having conquered the north and shortly after, most of China, he set up his capital in Nanking and married the daughter of one of Shanghai's richest bankers. By 1928 he had taken Peking.

In the process of success, Chiang had upset the communists who began to form a separate force under the leadership of Mao Tse-tung. Civil war was only deferred as a result of the attack from Japan in 1937. It was at this time that China ceased payment of its foreign loans together with interest as may be evidenced from the last coupons attached to each bond.

Four years after the Japanese war, the communists took full control and Chiang was expelled to Taiwan. Mao Tse-tung proclaimed the formation of the People's Republic of China on 1 October 1949.

THE LUNG-TSING-U-HAI RAILWAY

Earlier reference was made to the intention of quoting an example of the construction and financing methods of a major railway. The Lung-Tsing-U-Hai was one of the longest railways in the country and its story is typical of many of the lines built with foreign assistance.

Discussions between the National Assembly and the Belgian Compagnie Generale de Chemins de Fer et de Tramways en Chine, led to the signing of a loan agreement in September 1912 for £10 million. The purpose was to construct a major railway from Kansu to the sea. The actual route of the railway was from Lanchow-fu (the capital of Kansu province) to Haichow, a seaport. Two main sections were involved, the Pieulo and the Lo'tung.

The former ran between Loyang and Kaifeng and had been built by the Belgian Compagnie Generale in 1905 and financed by a Belgian Frs. 41 million loan raised in 1903 and subsequently repaid by the 1913 £10 million loan. In order to block further Belgian concessions, the acting Governor of Honan established the Lo'tung Railway Company which had the objective of constructing four major railways in the province linking up to form the Lo'tung section. Various methods were used to finance these sections, for example, owners of more than 50 mu (about one-seventh of an acre) had to buy a 5 Ti share for every 50 mu, and businesses with a capital of over 300 Taels had to buy one share, over 500 Taels, two shares, etc. Other more exotic pressures were exerted, such as surtaxes on salt and agriculture production, and a levy of 0.12 silver dollars on each ounce of opium produced.

But the effect was not as anticipated – progress was slow, and increasing local dissatisfaction led to riots, the most serious being the burning down of the company office at Huayin, together with local schools and telegraph poles – symbols of exploitation of the poor. Eventually the Government took control in 1911, and so began the discussions with Compagnie Generale on completion of the total railway.

Out of the £10 million authorized by the loan agreement of 1912 £4 million was issued to finance the Belgian construction work of the unfinished sections, £228,200 was used to repay advances and £292,180 was used to repay the 1907 Pieulo loan. The loan was secured by a prior charge on the net earnings of the railroad and was originally repayable over the forty years to 1953 by equal annual amounts. In 1936 a renegotiation resulted in the term being extended until 1982. Interest was paid until 1925, and the arrears between 1925 and 1936 were waived as part of the 1936 renegotiation. Interest was paid at $1\frac{1}{2}\%$ in 1937 and 2% in 1938, but no further payments were made.

The enormity of the project meant that further loans were required to complete the railroad and new loans were raised in 1920, 1921, 1923 and 1925.

A listing of other Chinese railway bonds is included at the end of this chapter.

WHAT CHANCE OF REPAYMENT?

With a relatively small amount of defaulted foreign debt (only £60 million versus Russia's £1,000 million) together with the coming of the country's second industrial revolution, the question of repayment is often raised. No one, of course, can be sure that China will ever feel obliged to repay, but continuing pressure is being applied on the country to settle up and who knows what may happen. One thing is certain and that is that if there is a settlement, the rarity of those bonds left in collectors' hands will increase dramatically.

COLLECTING FIELDS

Under the overall heading of China, there are several collecting themes. Only two have been referred to here, namely Railways and Government issues. These two are often intertwined, as the railways were usually government owned and thus their borrowings, government guaranteed. There are, however, three other sub-sections which may appeal. These are:

1 Internal Loans (usually only in Chinese and similar in size to banknotes)
2 Municipal Loans (particularly those of Shanghai)
3 Shares of companies operating in China or set up to finance the country's industrial development.

Chinese material has in the past been oversold. In time, repayment or not, it is the author's view that the bonds of this country will become the most desirable of all sectors.

SAMPLE LISTING OF CHINESE BONDS AND SHARES

Not intended as a comprehensive catalogue, the following gives some indication of material available to the collector. Reference numbers are from the Drumm & Henseler catalogue and, where known, numbers originally issued are shown. The 'outstanding' figure indicates the proportion of the total loan not redeemed at time of default. Retail prices range from £10 to £2,000 according to rarity but these should be obtained from leading dealers.

GOVERNMENT BONDS

1898 4½% Gold Loan

Cat. No.	Description	Den.	No. issued
ISSUED BY DEUTSCH-ASIATISCHE BANK			
CA 101 a	Red/Grey	£25	28,500
(Unissued)	Red/Grey	£25	Est. 45
CA 101 b	Orange/Lilac	£50	58,500
(Unissued)	Orange/Lilac	£50	Est. 45
CA 101 c	Brown/Pale Blue	£100	43,125
CA 101 d	Purple/Lilac	£500	100
ISSUED BY HONGKONG & SHANGHAI BANK			
CA 102 a	Red/Grey	£25	1,500
CA 102 b	Orange/Lilac	£50	1,500
CA 102 c	Brown/Pale Blue	£100	66,875
CA 102 d	Purple/Lilac	£500	2,400

Total Loan: £16,000,000, of which £2,996,425 remains outstanding.

1903 5% Emprunt Chinois

Cat. No.	Description	Den.	No. issued
CA 106	Dated 1905 (centre) with 2 large 'chops' Pink/Grey.	Frs 500	50,000
CA 107	Dated 1907 with only 1 'chop' on right.	Frs 500	32,000

Total Loan: Frs 41 million of which large part still outstanding.

1908 5% Imperial Chinese Government

Cat. No.	Description	Den.	No. issued
ISSUED BY HONGKONG & SHANGHAI BANK			
CA 114 a	Small format Green/Black, attractive vignette.	£20	5,000
CA 114 b	Mauve/Black.	£100	24,000
ISSUED BY BANQUE DE L'INDO CHINE			
CA 114 c	Green/Black, as 114 a. Bank in bottom left.	£20	125,000

Out of total issue £5,000,000, only 5% (£250,000) outstanding.

1912 5% Chinese Government Gold Loan (Crisp)

Cat. No.	Description	Den.	No. issued
CA 120 a	Blue/Yellow	£20	32,500
CA 120 b	Green/Black	£100	26,000
CA 120 c	Brown/Pale Blue	£500	2,000
CA 120 d	Red/White	£1,000	750

Total Issue: £5,000,000 of which £3,666,980 (73%) remains outstanding.

1913 5% Chinese Government Reorganization Loan

Cat. No.	Description	Den.	No. issued
ISSUED BY HONGKONG & SHANGHAI BANKING CORP.			
CA 126 a	Brown/Black	£20	95,834
CA 126 b	Blue/Black	£100	55,000
ISSUED BY DEUTSCH-ASIATISCHE BANK			
CA 126 c	Brown/Black	M. 409	120,000
CA 126 d	Blue/Black	M. 2045	36,000
ISSUED BY BANQUE DE L'INDO CHINE			
CA 126 e	Brown/Black	Frs 505	370,833
ISSUED BY RUSSO-ASIATISCHE BANK			
CA 126 f	Green/Black	Rbls 189.40	138,889

Total Issue: £25,000,000, of which £19,691,880 (79%) remains outstanding.

1918 8% Marconi Treasury Bills

Cat. No.	Description	Den.	No. issued
CA 136 a	Red/Yellow	£100	1,500
CA 136 b	Red/Yellow	£500	500
CA 136 c	Red/Yellow	£1,000	200

Total Issue: £600,000, all outstanding. Original interest rate of 8% later reduced. New coupon sheet attached.

1919 8% Vickers Treasury Notes

Cat. No.	Description	Den.	No. issued
CA 139 a	Green/Black	£100	9,082
As above, but original coupons		£100	—
CA 139 b	Blue/Black	£500	750
As above, but original coupons		£500	—
CA 139 c	Brown/Black	£1,000	520

Total Issue: £1,803,200, all of which remains outstanding.

1925 8% Skoda Loan

Cat. No.	Description	Den.	No. issued
CA 157 a	Brown/Blue/Black	£5	3,401
CA 157 b	Mauve/Blue/Black	£10	4,604
CA 157 c	Green/Blue/Black	£50	6,000
CA 157 d	Brown/Blue/Black	£100	6,030
CA 157 e	Orange/Blue/Black	£500	2,200
CA 157 f	Red/Blue/Black	£1,000	4,800

Total Issue: £6,866,046, all outstanding. This loan was used to repay the 1913 'Austrian' Loan.

1934 6% Indemnity Loan

Cat. No.	Description	Den.	No. issued
CA 201 a	Brown/Green w. portrait of Sun Yat-sen.	£50	2,000
CA 201 b	Green/Orange.	£100	4,000
CA 201 c	Red/Pink.	£1,000	1,000

Total Issue: £1,500,000 of which £972,000 remains outstanding.

RAILWAY ISSUES

1899 5% Chinese Imperial Railway

Cat. No.	Description	Den.	No. issued
CA 103	Large format in Brown/Pale Blue.	£100	23,000

Total Loan: £2,300,000 of which £172,500 remains outstanding (i.e. 1,725 bonds). Issued by the British & Chinese Corporation Ltd.

1903 5% Shanghai-Nanking Railway

CA 108	Long narrow in Pink/White. Serial nos. 1–7,500.	£100	7,500
CA 109	Same format. Serial nos. 7,501–15,000	£100	15,000
CA 110	Same format. Dated 1907 bottom left.	£100	6,500

Total Loan: £3,250,000 issued in three tranches of which £2,784,000 remains outstanding (86%).

1905 5% Honan Railway

CA 112	Large format Green/White with Yellow backdrop. Dated 1905 bottom left.	£100	7,000
CA 112 b	As above but dated 1906.	£100	1,000

Original issue of £700,000 increased to £800,000 (CA 112 b) £475,000 outstanding

Tientsin-Pukow Railway – 1908

ISSUED BY DEUTSCH ASIATISCHE BANK

CA 115 a	Lilac/Blue in German & Chinese.	£20	60,000
CA 115 b	Lilac/Green	£100	19,500

Total Issue: £3,150,000 of which £2,442,740 outstanding.

1911 5% Hukuang Railway

ISSUED BY HONGKONG & SHANGHAI BANKING CORP.

CA 117 a	Green/Black	£20	2,500
CA 117 b	Red/Black	£100	14,500

ISSUED BY DEUTSCH-ASIATISCHE BANK

CA 117 c	Green/Black	£20	30,000
CA 117 d	Red/Black	£100	9,000

ISSUED BY BANQUE DE L'INDO CHINE

CA 117 e	Green/Black	£20	37,500
CA 117 f	Red/Black	£100	7,500

ISSUED BY AMERICAN BANKS

CA 117 g	Green/Black	£20	150
CA 117 h	Red/Black	£100	14,970
As above but with revenue stamps		£100	—

Out of the total issue of £6,000,000, 94% (£5,656,000) remains outstanding. Apart from usual coupon clipping, all bonds have coupon numbers 52 and 54 missing.

1913 5% Lung-Tsing-U-Hai Railway

Cat. No.	Description	Den.	No. issued
CA 124	Blue/Black	£20	200,000
CA 124 a	As above but original coupons.	£20	
CA 124 b	As above but 'Belgian nos', i.e. serial nos from 220,000–240,000.	£20	
CA 124 c	Overprinted 'Duplicate'.	£20	
CA 124 d	Unissued reserve.	£20	Est. 1,400

Total issue of £4,000,000, all outstanding.

1936 6% Shanghai-Hangchow-Ningpo Railway

CA 205 a	Green/Black with Sun Yat-sen on front. View of bridge on reverse.	£50	6,000
CA 205 b	Brown/Black	£100	8,000

Total Issue: £1,100,000, all outstanding.

MISCELLANEOUS

Banque Industrielle de Chine

CA 301 a	Blue/Black	FF 500	3,000
CA 301 b	Yellow/Black	FF 500	87,000
CA 301 c	Yellow/Black	FF 500	60,000
CA 301 d	Yellow/Black	FF 500	150,000

Cie Generale de Chemins de Fer et de Tramways en Chine 1920

CA 303	Tan/Blue/Black	Frs 250	12,000

Chinese Engineering and Mining Co.

Bearer share certificate; den. 5 shares

Compagnie Financiere Belgo-Chinoise

Founders Shares; Red/Blue
50 Chinese $ Ordinary shares; Red/Blue; Action de capital

EUROPE

Perhaps more correctly entitled 'Continental Europe', this chapter concentrates on the historical development of the major industrial nations of France, Germany and the Low Countries. Reference to bonds and shares is relatively limited as collectors of these countries tend to be nationally rather than internationally concentrated. It is felt, however, that the Industrial Revolution and its progress through these areas, was of such importance to the development of modern companies with their resultant bond and share issues that a summary knowledge of the economic history of each country is essential for the enthusiastic scripophilist.

FRANCE

Perhaps, of all the European countries, with the possible exception of Spain, the certificates of France are the most decorative and for this reason, if not rarity, there is a steady demand for them. Most date from 1900 although it is possible to obtain items from the eighteenth century; shares in the Canal de Richelieu (1753) and the Mine de Plomb Tenant Argent à Lenards (1790) are fine examples. In order to provide a better understanding of French material, a brief history of the economic development of the country is provided below.

SUMMARY HISTORY

The Industrial Revolution began in Britain around the 1770s but did not reach France until after the end of the Napoleonic wars in 1815 and even then it was not until about 1830 that real progress in industrialization got under way.

The eighteenth century was broken up by wars and the Revolution, thus inhibiting the development of industry. The population was widely spread over the countryside and in 1700 only three towns (Paris, Lyons and Marseilles) exceeded 100,000 persons. Great emphasis was placed on family-owned and -run companies and little encouragement was provided by external financing bodies, although towards the end of the century some banks were created to try to fill this gap. The Caisse d'Escompte was one such operation which contributed substantial funds to the Société des Mines d'Anzin.

Domestic industrialization may have been lacking in the eighteenth century, but foreign trade certainly was not and business thrived on dealings with its colonies and continental partners. Textiles, the refining of sugar and vegetable oils and the manufacture of cheap trinkets for the purchase of slaves, were all active businesses – at least until the Revolution.

In 1808 three types of company were created:
1 The joint company (owner-managed and -financed)
2 The limited company (externally financed)
3 The company with shares, or joint-stock company.
Of these, the most common was the first example and most unusual the last. Regulations restricting joint-stock companies were so rigid, at least until 1867, that between 1815 and 1848 only 342 such companies were formed. This explains the dearth of early share certificates available for today's collector of French commercial enterprises. Those joint-stock companies formed were largely in the areas of coal mining, metallurgy, chemicals and textiles. One of the largest companies of the time (Creusot) was a 'limited' company.

Finance was mainly internally generated by each company although during the 1840s to 1850s numerous bond issues were made by companies, such as Decazeville in 1842, to finance replacement machinery.

Road transport was good, even during the eighteenth century and an effective canal system was

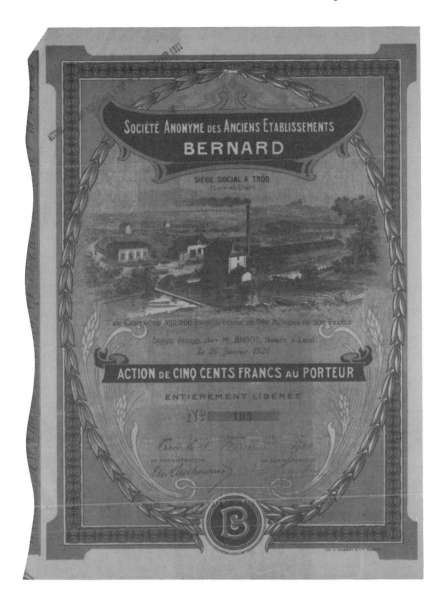

S.A. des Anciens Etablissements Bernard, 1920 bearer share of which only 700 were issued.

developed during the early part of the next. Early railways were only used for carrying coal from the mines to waiting barges and it was not until 1837 that the first passenger service was opened between Paris and St Germain. For comparison, in 1848 France had 1,800 km of railway open whilst each of Britain, Germany and Belgium exceeded 10,000 km. But once building was under way, progress was fast and there is no doubt that the growth of the railways greatly assisted the growth of heavy industry. As we will see in the later chapter on Automobiles, France led the world in the early commercial manufacture of vehicles around the turn of the century.

CERTIFICATES FOR THE COLLECTOR

Mention has already been made of the shortage of early industrial material. One sector of early certificates which is fairly readily available, however, are the 'Tontines' of 1780–1810. These were organizations formed by groups of individuals pooling their resources with the objective of the last surviving member winning the pot. Similar schemes began in England but were eventually made illegal due to the incentive for members to murder one another and so take the prize. The certificates often carry a number of elaborate signatures and no doubt each (as a unique document) could yield considerable interest to the researcher.

*Scenes of Paris surround this
attractive certificate of the
Omnibus of Paris of 1912.*

Other sectors of French material are:

Automobiles (see page 97)

Colonial companies

Banks

Entertainment (such as casinos and hotels)

Many are extremely attractive and their design, often by contemporary artists, tends to reflect the period of issue. With the exception of registered shares ('nominative'), in which it is illegal to deal in France, material is generally freely available, although the most attractive pieces are often difficult to obtain.

GERMANY

Having produced the first catalogues, Germany may be considered the birthplace of scripophily – certainly as far as commercialization is concerned. But it was not the national material which caught the imagination of budding collectors, but that of the more exotic Russia and China. This is not to say that German scrip was uncollected; in Germany itself there was, and still is, tremendous interest in this paper. For the outsider, however, there is not a widespread appeal for material of the nineteenth century. The reasons for this are largely twofold; one – it is unattractive, and two – it is usually written in German only, and old German at that. For the enthusiast, however, these reasons should not be a deterrent, for the qualities of rarity and historical interest are still very much present in this sector, and these combine with a developed home market to produce a most interesting collecting theme.

As in the previous section on France, a brief background to the economic development of the country is provided below.

SUMMARY HISTORY

Britain led the way with early industrialization and both France and Germany were slow to follow. Of the two, Germany was the slower, for three main reasons.

1 In 1789 the country was divided into as many as 314 independent territories. National unification was not achieved until 1871.
2 Its geographical location resulted in regular involvement in European wars and acted as a buffer between eastern and western Europe.
3 Transport systems were poor until well into the nineteenth century.

Until the arrival of steam traction, industry was almost non-existent and the population was ninety per cent rural. This changed rapidly after the building of the first railway from Nürnberg to Fürth in 1835. This short line was followed by the longer Leipzig – Dresden Railway in 1839 and during the 1840s over 100 million Talers were invested in shares and debentures of the railway companies. Amongst the many lines constructed, the major ones were:

Munich–Augsburg　1840
Cologne–Aachen　1843
Berlin–Hamburg　1846
Cologne–Minden　1847

All were privately controlled, although the Prussian government subsidized approximately half of the total investment. The greatest benefit of the lines was the improved transport of coal, thus generating further industry particularly on the large coal and iron fields. Between 1850 and 1875, most railway companies were purchased by the State for economic or strategic reasons and the business continued to be very profitable.

Development of an infrastructure was not limited to railways, and both canals and roads were actively constructed. Many of the new roads were owned privately and operated a toll system (very like the US 'turnpikes'); an example is the Mecklenburg–Strelitz road which continued to charge users until 1915.

Much of the business of Germany was domestic and it was not until the latter part of the nineteenth century that much attention was paid to international trade. At that time several banks were formed to encourage such expansion, for example, the Deutsche–Asiatische Bank in 1889, and the Deutsche–Überseebank in 1886. The major German banks, such as Deutsche and Dresdener, were formed in the early 1870s, and a close relationship with industry developed from a very early date. This close involvement continues to the present day and apart from Japan, is unusual in the capitalist world. Involvement not only entails lending but also common directorships and minority shareholdings.

The most significant date in recent history is 1871, for not only was Germany 'unified' but it also standardized its currency. Until that date, seven different silver currencies, based on Taler or Gulden, existed. These were replaced by the gold Mark, thus joining Britain in adopting the gold standard. These currency changes are clearly reflected in the bonds and shares of the period.

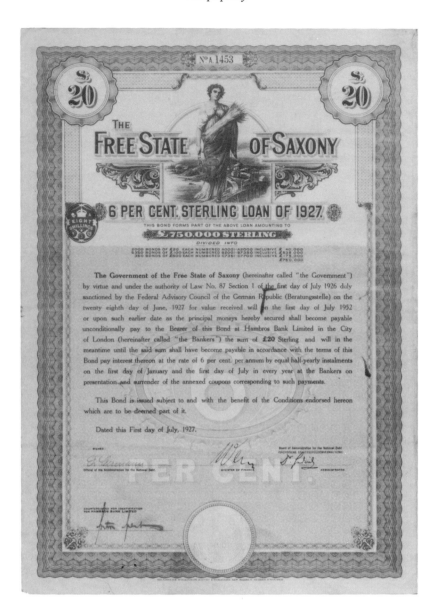

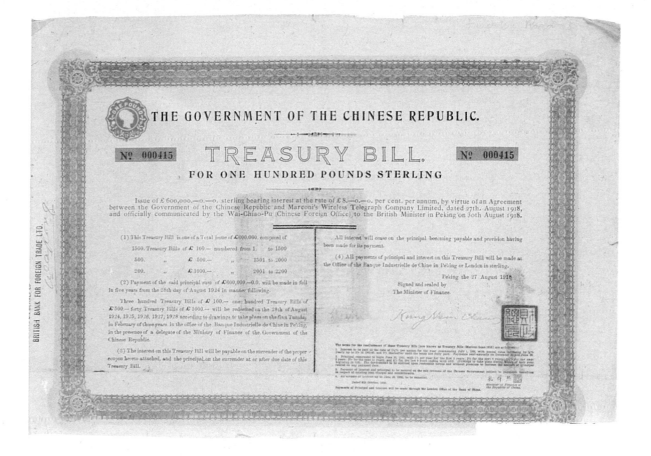

THE GOVERNMENT OF THE CHINESE REPUBLIC.

Nº 000415 TREASURY BILL. Nº 000415

FOR ONE HUNDRED POUNDS STERLING

Opposite: *Free State of Saxony £20 bond of 1927 – only 2,000 were issued.*

Above: *A Chinese Government £100 Treasury Bill dated 1918 to finance imports from the Marconi Company: only 1,500 of this type were issued.*

Left: *A Banque Industrielle de Chine bearer share.*

Opposite: *The Shanghai Electric Construction Co. Unissued share c. 1935. This company was liquidated and shareholders paid out in the 1950–60s.*

Left: *£100 bond of the City of Dresden, 1927.*

LATER DEVELOPMENTS AND CERTIFICATES

Following the intensive period of industrial growth, the end of the nineteenth century saw the building of many towns together with the associated services of electricity, tramways and retail businesses.

Local state and municipal financing continued well into this century and two loans in particular warrant some comment; the City of Dresden and the Free State of Saxony were both issued in 1927 but as they now fall in the Democratic Republic, both remain defaulted. Considerable efforts have been made to obtain settlement but so far without success. The bonds are, however, very attractive, written in English and of fairly low issue, thus of benefit to the collector if not the original investor! Several other loans of the 1930s remain in default, particularly the so-called 'Young Loans'; these are expected to be settled on resolution of the exchange rate aspects.

BELGIUM

Well-endowed with enormous reserves of coal and iron combined with the presence of a natural waterway system aiding both transport and power, Belgium was able to take full and speedy advantage of the industrial revolution. A long history of industrial involvement laid the ground rules for an even greater development. The first limited company was formed in 1835 – 'S.A. Hauts Fournaux, Usines et Charbonnage de Marcinelle et Couillet', a vast organization involved in iron and coal mining, blast furnaces and rolling mills.

The major banks of Société General and the Bank of Belgium often took controlling interests in many of the companies of the time, leaving only small shareholdings in the hands of the general public. The company 'La Providence' for example had only ten to twenty outside shareholders. Foreign capital was supplied by the Rothschilds and others, and the intense activity soon established Belgium as one of the foremost industrial countries of Europe. Plans for the construction of the first and most concentrated railway network in the world were presented as early as 1830 and it was not long before Belgium became, with Britain, a major exporter of railway equipment, as is evidenced by the many Chinese railways built and financed by them, the Lung-Tsing-U-Hai Railway is a typical example.

Textiles had for many years been an important industry, but with the arrival of steam, the business was actively developed. Initially drawing ideas and equipment from Britain (indeed, Lievin Bauwens imported a whole factory including workers) the natural innovation and inventiveness of the people soon improved production techniques.

Many of the share certificates available to collectors today relate to the basic industries of coal, iron and textiles, but many others exist, particularly the early railway and canal companies and the municipal authorities, such as the City of Antwerp $2\frac{1}{2}$% Loan of 1887.

HOLLAND

Considering the proximity of the two countries, it is perhaps surprising how widely they differ. Industrial revolution came late to Holland and whereas Belgium was able to build on substantial mineral resources and a long history of industrialization, Holland was quite the opposite with most of its businessmen traditionally involved in shipping and commerce.

The Dutch East India Company is perhaps the most famous reminder of the influence of the country on foreign trade and colonization, but in 1803 the only companies in existence which may have been classed 'industrial', were a rifle factory at Kuilerburg, a textile business at Amsterdam, a glass works at Leerdam, and fourteen sugar beet factories. Sugar refining and diamond cutting were the two early industries of any significance, the latter being established in Amsterdam in 1822.

Railway construction was slow, and in 1850 the country could only boast 170 km of track versus Belgium's 861 km. The first line was built between Amsterdam and Haarlem in 1839, more emphasis being placed on waterways and shipping.

Early certificates of this country are relatively scarce as it was not until 1863 that limited liability companies were authorized by the Government. Those items which do exist are of primary interest to the local market.

OTHER COUNTRIES OF EUROPE

Space considerations unfortunately limit the amount of further time which can be devoted to Continental Europe. Regrettably this means that such fascinating countries as Spain, Austria, Italy and Switzerland are omitted. This is certainly not a reflection on the quality of material available from these countries; Spain in particular issued a number of extremely decorative and rare certificates from as early as 1749 and Switzerland boasts a number of attractive and unusual pieces relating to mountain railways and hotels amongst other industrial issues. Our apologies to enthusiasts of these countries but perhaps further works will give them a more deserving write up.

GREAT BRITAIN

THE INDUSTRIAL REVOLUTION

Despite the frenzied industrial activity of France and Belgium, there is little doubt that the Industrial Revolution began in Britain. An exact date is difficult to specify, but economic historians tend to agree on a period around the 1770s–1780s. The forty years or so prior to this period prepared the ground and three principal factors have been identified:

1 The development of international markets, particularly through colonialization and improved reliablity of shipping transportation
2 A period of unusually good agricultural harvests
3 An increase in overall population.

The catalysts required to convert these factors into revolution took the form of a burst of inventions together with the construction of roads and canals. The inventions, such as Arkwright's water frame, Hargreave's Spinning Jenny and Watt's steam engine, had an enormous effect on the cotton and iron industries and it was the latter which previously had been suffering from lack of fuel (having relied on local forests) which was able to benefit most from improved transport enabling cheaper deliveries of coal to steel areas. Thus Coalbrookdale's Iron Bridge became a milestone in the progress of industry. Built in 1779, the bridge was the first cast iron construction of its kind.

By 1760, as many as seventeen coke blast furnaces existed in the country and in the latter part of the eighteenth century the proportion of population living in towns increased from sixteen to twenty-five per cent. There is no doubt that Britain benefited from the political revolution going on in Europe and the United States, permitting it to consolidate an already international economic position but, above all else, the most significant factor which turned the Industrial Revolution into a long-term phase of progress was the building of the railways.

THE RAILWAYS

A future chapter deals with this subject in rather more detail than is intended here, but in view of the significance of railways in the country's development, and also in the material available to the scripophilist, it is impossible to move on without some comment.

It was not until 1825 that the world's first commercial railway was opened running between Stockton and Darlington, but the greatest expansion occurred in the 'mania' periods of 1836–7 and post-1850. In 1843, 2,000 miles of track was in existence and by 1867, this had risen to over 12,000 miles. Not only did the railway companies take away the trade of the old Turnpike Trusts and Canal Companies (by 1865 one-third of all canals were under the direct control of the railway companies), but they permitted a rapid expansion in industrialization. Associated businesses supplying rails, bricks and equipment all thrived generating an enormous injection of funds into the economy.

Right: *The Herne Bay Steam Packet Co., an attractive, early British certificate of 1837.*

Below: *Very early and rare certificate in the Newry Navigation Co. Printed on vellum, 1834.*

Left: *The Thames & Severn Canal Navigation of 1794.*

Below: *The Metropolitan Saloon Omnibus Co. Ltd – an early forerunner of London Transport, the company was formed in 1856 and was the first to use covered vehicles.*

The increased mobility of resources, with labour and capital, completely transformed the country. The redistribution of wealth prompted the Duke of Wellington to complain that railways 'enabled the lower orders to go uselessly wandering about the country'.

The initial enthusiasm for the early railways has shown little abatement over the years and the subject is an extremely popular one for scripophilists. But although there were a great many British railway companies formed during the nineteenth century, many were controlled by relatively small groups of investors, thus limiting the initial number of originally issued share certificates. The availability of material is further hampered by the groupings of the early twentieth century and their eventual full nationalization. As a result of this process, most certificates were handed in to the head offices, such as Great Northern and Great Western. Initially these were no doubt kept in registers but over time, many have been lost, spoiled or destroyed. Despite this, certificates are around and the collector can have great fun building up a collection at the right price.

COMPANY FINANCING

Following the collapse of the South Sea Company in 1720 the government, through the passing of the 'Bubble Act', prohibited the formation of joint-stock limited liability companies unless specifically authorized by Act of Parliament. This position continued until the limited liability acts of the 1850s and greatly restricted the number of such companies formed during that period. Not all were put off by the lengthy process of authorization, however, but such companies were largely limited to the Turnpike Trusts and Canal Companies. As a result many small savers invested in Canal shares, which around the 1790s experienced something of a boom.

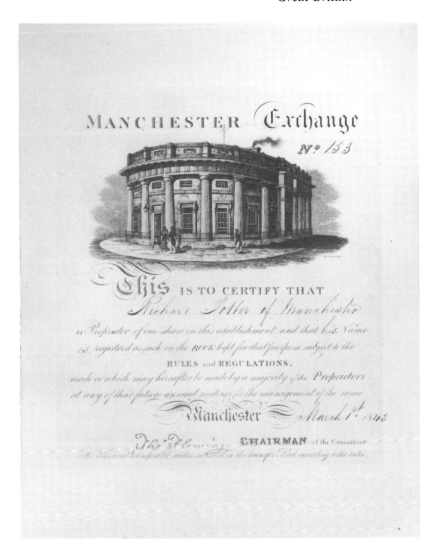

The next change in legislation affecting limited liability companies did not come until the beginning of the twentieth century when further easing of the rules resulted in the formation of numerous ventures, many with exotic sounding names and little else. The financing of the nineteenth-century railway companies is dealt with in more detail on pages 83–9.

COLLECTING GREAT BRITAIN

Inevitably, in view of its relative importance, a disproportionate amount of this chapter has been devoted to railways. This should not imply that this is the only worthwhile collecting theme within this sector. Indeed there are many earlier companies formed to build bridges, theatres, libraries and sporting facilities, which offer the collector a wide variety of high-quality material. Many of these institutions were financed by small groups of local businessmen and the certificates are often extremely attractive, bearing vignettes and fine seals, and occasionally printed on vellum. Several have been referred to in the ensuing summary, but the collector must expect to pay rather more for this level of quality and a collection based on pre-1830 items will be costly and difficult to assemble.

For the lighter minded scripophilist, however, there are a vast number of different share certificates covering all possible fields of interest. Most are of this century and consequently inexpensive.

Choosing 'Britain' as a collecting theme is thus a vast arena but in view of its importance in the development of world industrialization, the results bring economic history to life.

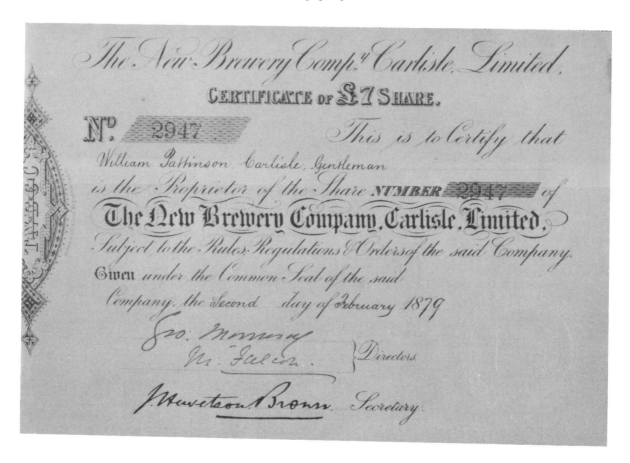

Above: *The New Brewery Co. of Carlisle. Formed in 1879 the company was nationalized in 1916 in order to control local alcoholism affecting a munitions factory.*

Right: *The Wesleyan Proprietary Grammar School of 1838.*

Opposite: *The Northern Coal Mining Co. Unusual early English share certificate with fine vignettes, 1837.*

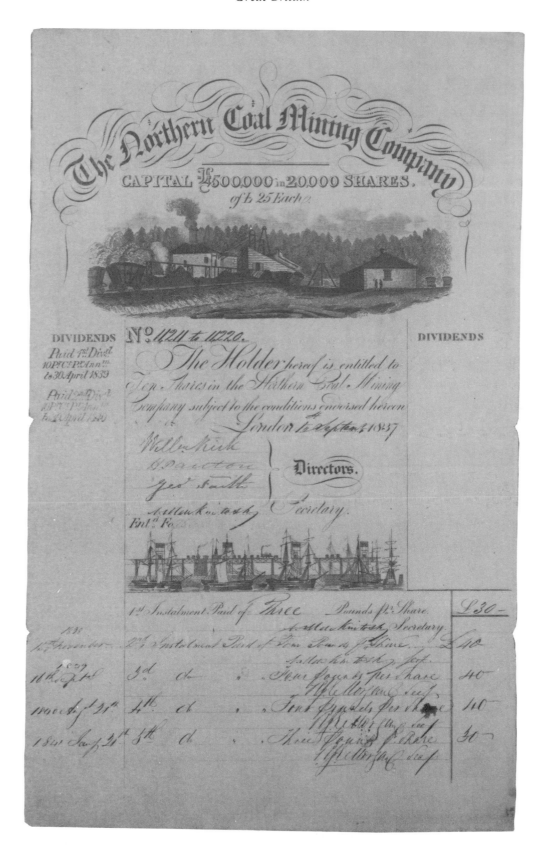

Right: *Share certificate in the Theatre Royal Drury Lane showing the interior layout. The Theatre was burned down and funds were raised to rebuild it.*

Below: *The Anglo-Belgian Co. of Egypt showing views of the pyramids – it was engraved by Bradbury, Wilkinson.*

A SAMPLE LISTING OF BRITISH MATERIAL

COMPANIES

Anglo-Belgian Co. of Egypt Ltd
£5 bond dated 1908. Green/Black with attractive vignette of train, with pyramid in background.

Annuities
Consolidated 3%, 1834–47
Reduced 3%, 1835

Bakou Consolidated Oil Fields, 1943
Certificate for 'A' Ordinary shares; Pink/Black
Certificate for 'B' Ordinary shares; Green/Black

Canterbury Navigation & Sandwich Harbour Co.
Superb early certificate of 1826 with vignette of cathedral and harbour scene.

Caldbeck Fells Consolidated Lead & Copper Mining Co. Ltd
Certificate for 5 shares. Dated 1870.
Early Northumberland mining company.
Capital £60,000 in 30,000 shares of £2 each. Black/White.

Coal Consumers Association Ltd
£1 share, 1873. Small vignette of coalman and customer shaking hands.

The Common Fund Co. Ltd
Scrip certificate for 100 £20 shares, dated 1869.

Cornish Clay & Tin Works
8,000 shares of £1 each. Capitalized by Certificate for 1 share dated 1864 in Blue/Black

Dublin Distillers Co. Ltd
Capital £100,000. Share of £300, dated 1929.

East Indian Iron Co.
£10 share certificate. Dated 1854. Embossed seal.

Liverpool Imperial Loan & Investment Co.
Certificate for 1 share in this early company. Dated 1847 with vignette of 'liver bird' and Red embossed seal.

London & Globe Finance Corp. Ltd
£1 bond, 1895.

Louise & Co. Ltd
Capital £163,000; bearer certificate for 1 founder share (3,000 issued).

Nova Scotia Land & Gold Crushing
£2 share dated 1863. Heraldic vignette.

Oriental Hotels Company Ltd
£10 share of 1863 with embossed seal of elephant.

The Ottoman Company Ltd
Bearer share for £20 dated 1865. Very attractive certificate printed by Bradbury Wilkinson & Co. Vignettes of palm tree, camel & Turk, with minarets in background; embossed seal of shields and flag. The company lasted only 9 months, and was formed to trade with the Ottoman Empire.

The South Wales United Collieries Ltd
Bearer share certificate for 5 shares with coupons. Large format. Green/Black. Attractive design. Capital £125,000 in £1 shares. Dated c. 1908.

Strand Bridge
Certificate for 1 share dated 1809. Printed on vellum with gold seal and embossed view of bridge.

Watney Combe Reid & Co. Ltd
3½% perpetual first debenture stock. Vignette of stag & embossed seal of stag. Dated 1922.
Large attractive certificate for £100 debenture redeemable 1956–68, dated 1942.

Wellingborough Corn Exchange Co.
Capital £5,000. £25 share dated 1858. Sheaf of corn & farming implements in embossed seal.

William Barningham & Co. Ltd Pendleton Iron Works
3,000 shares. £20 share, dated 1874.

West Cumberland Iron & Steel Co. Ltd
Certificate for 1 share. Dated 1872. Capital £600,000 in 24,000 shares of £5 each. Black/White.

RAILWAYS

Ayr & Maybole Junction Railway Co.
£10 share certificate; attractive, decorative vignette; dated 1863.

The Border Counties Railway Company
Certificate for 5 shares. Black/White with Green overprint and embossed seal. c. 1855.

The Cornwall Railway
Certificate of £50 share. Black/Green. Embossed seal & watermarked paper. c. 1846.

Fishguard and Rosslare Railways & Harbour Co.
Preferred share certificate in Black/White dated 1904–1930.

The Guernsey Railway Company Ltd
Preference share certificate. c. 1943.

Greenock & Ayrshire Railway Co.
£10 share certificate. c. 1860.

Great Northern Railway Co.
Share certificate for £25, dated 1846. Coat-of-arms; embossed seal.

The Hull and Selby Railway Company
£12.10s share certificate. Attractive coat-of-arms. Dated 1845.

Leominster & Bromyard Railway Co.
Certificate of £10 share. Black/White. Embossed seal of early train. c. 1881.

Liverpool Overhead Railway Co.
£10 shares dated c. 1896. Vignette of overhead railway; Red & Pink with embossed seal.

Milford Haven Railway & Estate Co. Ltd
6% Perpetual Preference Shares. Certificate of 5 shares at £100 each. Dated 1882.

Paisley Barrhead & Hurlet Railway
Certificate for 5 shares. Black/White. c. 1846.

Tees Valley Railway Co.
£6 preference share. Dated 1875.

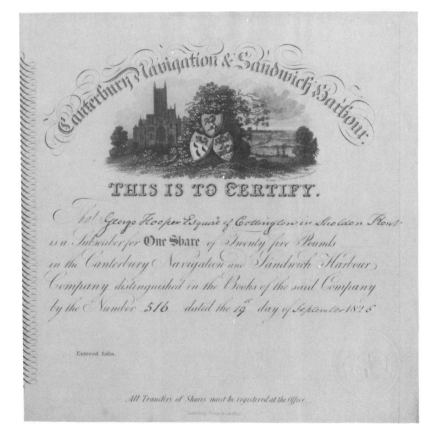

Above: *Formed to trade with the Ottoman Empire, the Ottoman Company lasted only nine months before liquidation. The certificate was engraved by Bradbury, Wilkinson.*

Right: *The Canterbury Navigation & Sandwich Harbour – very early English certificate of 1826, finely engraved and unusually attractive.*

Opposite: *The Cornwall Railway share certificate dated 1846 at the time of formation – it was absorbed into the Great Western in 1888.*

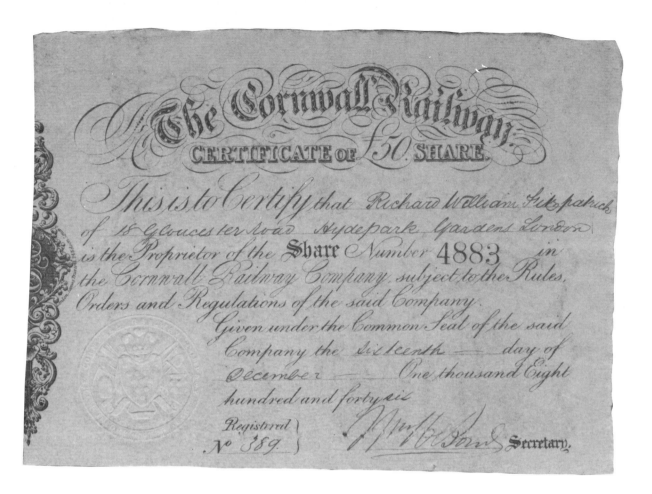

The Cornwall Railway

CERTIFICATE OF £50 SHARE.

This is to Certify that Richard William Fitzpatrick of 18 Gloucester Road Hydepark Gardens London is the Proprietor of the Share Number 4883 in the Cornwall Railway Company, subject to the Rules, Orders and Regulations of the said Company.

Given under the Common Seal of the said Company the Sixteenth day of December One thousand Eight hundred and fortysix

Registered } Nº 389 }

Secretary.

RUSSIA

The sheer vastness of the country with its multi-lingual and multi-religious peoples added considerable delays to the coming of the industrial revolution to Russia. Development was further hindered by the effects of serfdom, and despite considerable efforts by the government, particularly Count Ye. F. Kankrin (Minister of Finance 1823–44), Russia's economy was static and her share of world trade in 1850 was unchanged from that in 1800.

In the late eighteenth century, the country was one of the main producers of pig-iron thanks to the mines of the Urals, but over the next fifty years was rapidly overtaken by Britain, Germany and the United States. Russia's eventual defeat in the Crimean War (1853–6) emphasized its economic and social backwardness. Following this, considerable efforts were made, especially by Tsar Nicolas I, to eliminate serfdom, and the Peasants Land Bank was set up in 1882 to assist in the transfer of land from the nobility. The 1870s saw a rapid development of railways and the start of oil exploration at Baku.

By the end of the century a major metallurgical industry was established in the Ukraine based on the ore of Krivoy Rog and the coal of the Donetz basin. In 1897 Russia was put on the gold standard thus encouraging foreign investors. The French and Belgians primarily invested in the metallurgical industries of the south, while Britain concentrated on oil and Germany on electricity. Share certificates and bonds of the period clearly reflect this internationally segregated development.

SIGNIFICANCE TO SCRIPOPHILY

In order to appreciate the significance of Russia to the scripophilist, it is necessary to understand the enormity of the default which occurred in 1917 following the Revolution.

The overall lack of internal technological expertise combined with a social structure little changed from the Middle Ages, meant that development could only come with the aid of foreigners, both technocrats and financiers. Creating an infrastructure from nothing and catering for the consequent shift in demographic behaviour, with peasants moving from the fields to towns, required vast amounts of capital.

At the time of default well over £1,000 million in foreign bonds was outstanding. This position remains unchanged, thus placing Russia firmly in the number one slot for bad debtors. The bonds fall into three main categories although there is some overlap regarding state guarantees which were often applied to privately-owned railway company issues. The categories are:

  State loans
  Railways
  Cities

A further category is the many companies, usually joint ventures set up to develop the country. Most were privately owned and were ruined as a consequence of the Revolution.

Over sixty railway companies and twenty-eight cities issued foreign bonds. Of the cities, Moscow was the most prolific, with at least forty-three different issues, although many were replacements for earlier loans. Of the State issues, that of 1906 was the largest, with almost £86 million still outstanding. Needless to say, the number of bonds issued, in denominations ranging from £20 (or its equivalent) to £1,000, is quite enormous, but even so individual issues can often be quite small such as the 1912 City of Nicolaiev 2nd issue which amounted to only £41,620 in total.

The largest holdings of Tsarist bonds were in France and Germany, but following their default and the subsequent World Wars, a great many were lost or destroyed. Certainly most of the internal issues were destroyed in Russia itself. One might be forgiven for wondering why so many foreigners invested as heavily as they did in Russia. There are, perhaps, three main reasons:

1 Interest rates were higher than comparable 'gilt edged' securities and the bonds usually carried the government's guarantee.
2 The railway companies of Europe had proved to be profitable investments in their early days – similar successes were anticipated from the Russian companies.
3 The close links existing between Russian and European nobility gave encouragement by adding a reassuring touch.

But let us turn again to the internal developments of the country and more specifically the growth of the railways, which of all the major sectors offers the collector the greatest challenge and interest.

THE RAILWAYS

Development lagged behind Europe and America and it was only thanks to the enthusiasm and determination of Tsar Nicolas I that any progress was made at all. The first line, it is true, had little strategic or functional benefit, but it did at least provide a link from St Petersburg to the summer palace at Tsarskoye-Selo, now known as Pushkin and the birthplace of Alexander II. The line was opened in 1837 but it was not until the following year that steam traction was exclusively used. At that time, it was also extended to Pavlovsk – an entertainment resort holding concerts by such notables as Johann Strauss who, in 1860, was resident band-leader.

The next two lines to be approved for building were the Warsaw–Vienna Railway and the St Petersburg–Moscow Railway, which was subsequently sold to the Grand Russian Railway Company. These lines were of a more practical nature than Tsarskoye–Selo. Indeed, the Warsaw–Vienna line, which was finished in 1848, was put to a very practical use – it was used to transport troops to quell the Hungarian uprising.

FINANCIAL SKULDUGGERY

The government was unable to agree a single course of action in dealing with the building and financing of the railways. The net effect was of considerable benefit to the entrepreneurial constructors as the government invariably ended up bearing most of the financial responsibility.

The usual procedure was as follows; the constructor would be granted concessions to build a line, based on estimated costs, on which the share capital was determined. This cost was considerably in excess of the actual cost, which was met almost entirely from the sale of government guaranteed bonds, leaving the concessionaires with the bulk of the inflated share capital for which they had paid virtually nothing. There were even further opportunities for the promoters, for in addition to guaranteeing the interest and payment of the bonds, the government also guaranteed the dividends on the shares. It was therefore advantageous to the owners to reduce the operating profits as much as possible by spending the profits on expensive rolling stock (orders for which often resulted in payment of 'commissions') and maintenance. This increased the value of the property (and hence the value of the shares) but still the government-guaranteed dividends came rolling in.

Eventually the construction of the lines was taken on directly by the government, with the intention of selling them, when completed, to private concerns. The proceeds, invested in the government's new 'Railway Fund', were intended to finance the construction of further new lines.

The Railway Fund was initially financed by selling Alaska to the USA and then by selling shares of the various existing railway lines owned by the government. These included the Kursk–Kiev and Nicolas Railways. To supplement the income from the sale of lines that the government then built, Consolidated bond issues were raised by the government in Europe from 1870 to 1884. The effect of replacing the growing number of individual bond issues with the Coordinated and less frequent Consolidated loans helped restore foreign confidence in the Russian economy.

1869 Moscow-Smolensk 200 Thaler bond. One of the few Russian railway bonds to depict a train.

But the drain on the Fund of constructing all these new lines was such that, by 1880, the government only owned about thirty-five miles of operative railway line in the whole of the country. The only thing the government had to show for its denationalization programme was eighty per cent of the railway companies' debt.

LATER DEVELOPMENT

The great financial drain on the economy continued until 1884 when the government reversed its policy and began buying the private railways. A popular method was to exchange state guaranteed bonds in the name of the company for the share certificates. Examples of these bonds are as follows (catalogue numbers in parentheses):

Morschansk–Sysran	3% 1889	(1039)
Donetz	4% 1893	(1012)
Dvinsk–Witebsk	4% 1894	(1013)
Kursk–Kharkov–Azov	4% 1894	(1034)
Orel–Vitebsk	4% 1894	(1099)
Riga–Dvinsk	4½% 1894	(1103)
Transcaucasian	5% 1890	(1149)

Significantly the border designs of most of these bonds are identical.

The profitable companies that could not be taken over were encouraged to amalgamate with one another to create fewer, but larger, companies. Those formed in this way included: Riazan–Uralsk, South Eastern, Moscow–Kazan, Moscow–Kiev–Voronesh and the Moscow–Vindava–Rybinsk.

By 1900, these companies, together with the Chinese Eastern, Vladikavkas, Warsaw-Vienna, and Lodz Factory railways, owned more than ninety-five per cent of the mileage of the private railways, which represented thirty per cent of the total; the balance of seventy per cent being owned by the government. The companies that were swallowed up in this period of amalgamation included: Riazan–Koslov, Koslov–Voronesh–Rostov and Orel–Griasi.

From 1883 to 1905, while this policy of nationalization and amalgamation was being pursued, the government thwarted the creation of new private companies by refusing to guarantee their bond issues. However, from 1905, new companies were allowed to build short lines, several of which, on completion, were taken over by existing companies. Between 1909 and 1913, the number of private companies doubled to twenty-two. Some of the newly-formed companies, including those that were subsequently taken over, were:

Akkerman	(1001)	Oraienbaum	(1096)
Altai	(1002)	Podolisk	(1101, 1102)
Armavir–Tuapse	(1003, 1004)	Black Sea	(1122, 1123)
Herby–Kelzy	(1025)	Black Sea Kuban	(1121)
Eisk	(1028)	Semiretchensk	(1124)
Kahetian	(1029)	Tauris	(1145)
Kokand–Namangan	(1031)	Tockmack	(1146)
Koltchouguino	(1030)	Troitzk	(1150, 1151)
North Donetz	(1090, 1093)	West Ural	(1158)
North East Ural	(1094)	Wolmar	(1177)

CITY LOANS

The number of Russian cities and the quantity of bonds issued by them is appreciably lower than those of the railways and the State. Because of this they make an interesting collecting theme which is both achieveable (*vis-à-vis* quantity of variations) and rare.

Many issues were extremely small; mention having already been made of the City of Nicolaiev 2nd issue of which there were only fourteen of the £500 bonds issued. In addition they are also attractive. They rarely carry views of the city (Kharkov being an exception) but they invariably portray the municipal crest. In the case of Moscow, for example, this was St George slaying the dragon – as may be seen in the illustration on page 57.

The Soc. Minière Joltaia-Rieka (Krivoi Rog). A Belgian company operating in the heart of the Russian iron and steel area.

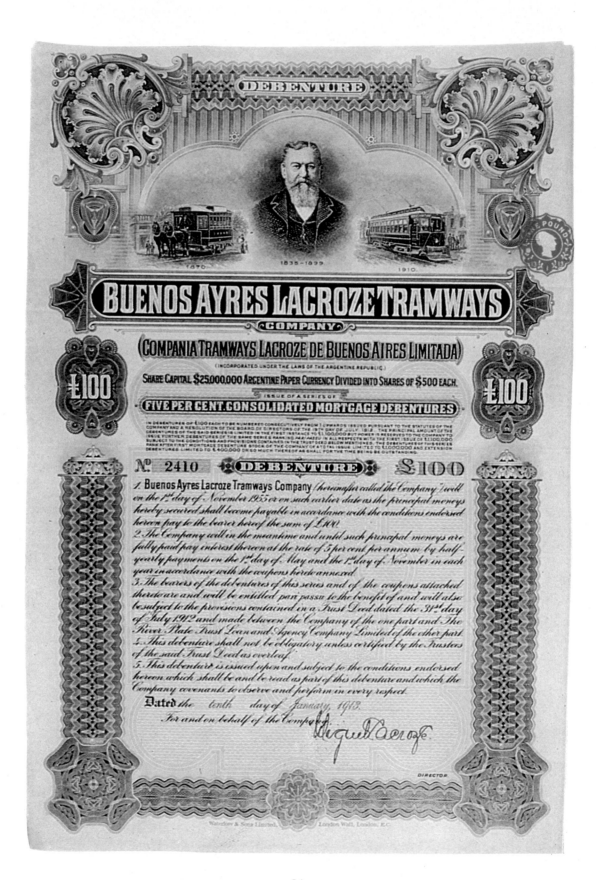

Opposite: *£100 debenture in the Buenos Ayres Lacroze Tramways Co. showing a vignette and signature of the founder. It was engraved by Waterlow.*

Left: *The Brazil Railway Co. £100 Gold Bond of 1909 – a typical example of Waterlow engraving.*

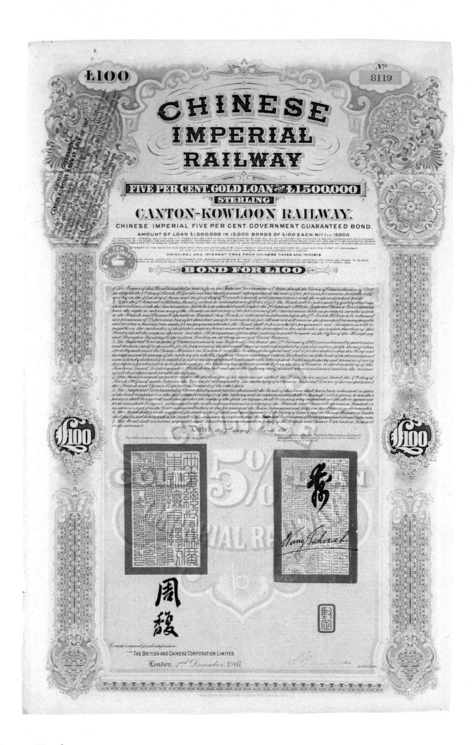

Above: *A Canton-Kowloon
Railway bond for £100 issued in
1907. The railway is now being
rebuilt.*

Opposite: *£20 bond of the City
of Moscow, 1908, showing the
city coat of arms – St George
slaying the dragon.*

Right: *A City of Vilna bond, one of those redeemed by the 1969 settlement.*

Opposite: *The Republic of Estonia, £100 bond of 1927, also repaid under the 1969 settlement.*

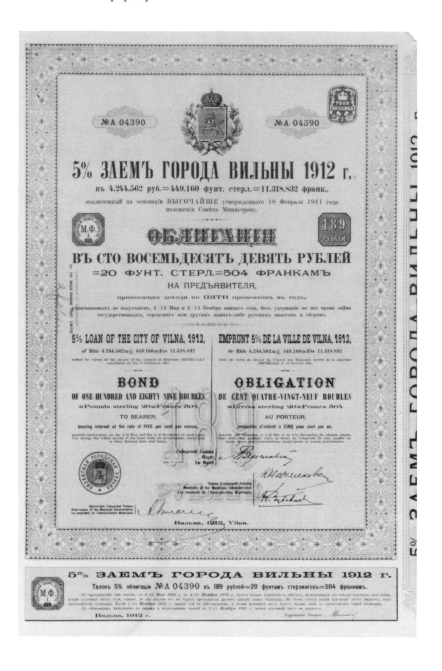

Not all 'Russian' bonds remained defaulted, however, and the saga of the Baltic State bonds makes interesting reading.

THE BALTIC STATES

Following the devastation of the First World War, the independent states of Estonia, Latvia and Lithuania proceeded to rebuild their ruined economies. The populace collected gold and other assets to the value of £5.7 million and deposited these with the Bank of England.

By 1940, all three states had been annexed by Russia, which then proceeded to dispose of or disperse most of the population. Germany occupied the territories a year later, at which point Britain impounded the Baltic assets by invoking the 'Trading with the Enemy' Act. With the final expulsion of Germany from Eastern Europe, Russia once more seized the three countries and demanded the return of the Baltic assets.

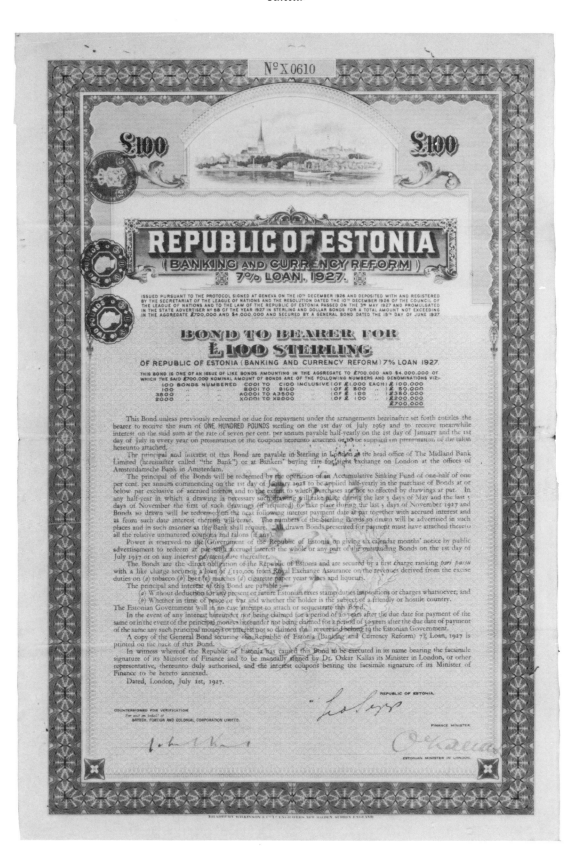

No. X 0610

£100   £100

REPUBLIC OF ESTONIA
(BANKING AND CURRENCY REFORM)
7% LOAN, 1927.

ISSUED PURSUANT TO THE PROTOCOL SIGNED AT GENEVA ON THE 10TH DECEMBER 1926 AND DEPOSITED WITH AND REGISTERED BY THE SECRETARIAT OF THE LEAGUE OF NATIONS AND THE RESOLUTION DATED THE 10TH DECEMBER 1926 OF THE COUNCIL OF THE LEAGUE OF NATIONS AND TO THE LAW OF THE REPUBLIC OF ESTONIA PASSED ON THE 3RD MAY 1927 AND PROMULGATED IN THE STATE ADVERTISER No 58 OF THE YEAR 1927 IN STERLING AND DOLLAR BONDS FOR A TOTAL AMOUNT NOT EXCEEDING IN THE AGGREGATE £700,000 AND $4,000,000 AND SECURED BY A GENERAL BOND DATED THE 18TH DAY OF JUNE 1927

BOND TO BEARER FOR
£100 STERLING
OF REPUBLIC OF ESTONIA (BANKING AND CURRENCY REFORM) 7% LOAN 1927.

THIS BOND IS ONE OF AN ISSUE OF LIKE BONDS AMOUNTING IN THE AGGREGATE TO £700,000 AND $4,000,000 OF WHICH THE SAID £700,000 NOMINAL AMOUNT OF BONDS ARE OF THE FOLLOWING NUMBERS AND DENOMINATIONS VIZ:-

100 BONDS NUMBERED	C001 TO	C100 INCLUSIVE	(OF £1,000 EACH)	£100,000
100	B001 TO	B100	(OF £ 500	£ 50,000
3500	A0001 TO	A3500	(OF £ 100	£350,000
2000	X0001 TO	X2000	(OF £ 100	£200,000
				£700,000

This Bond unless previously redeemed or due for repayment under the arrangements hereinafter set forth entitles the bearer to receive the sum of ONE HUNDRED POUNDS sterling on the 1st day of July 1967 and to receive meanwhile interest on the said sum at the rate of seven per cent. per annum payable half-yearly on the 1st day of January and the 1st day of July in every year on presentation of the coupons hereunto attached or to be supplied on presentation of the talon hereunto attached.

The principal and interest of this Bond are payable in Sterling in London at the head office of The Midland Bank Limited (hereinafter called "the Bank") or at Bankers' buying rate for sight exchange on London at the offices of Amsterdamsche Bank in Amsterdam.

The principal of the Bonds will be redeemed by the operation of an Accumulative Sinking Fund of one-half of one per cent. per annum commencing on the 1st day of January 1928 to be applied half-yearly in the purchase of Bonds at or below par exclusive of accrued interest and to the extent to which purchases are not so effected by drawings at par. In any half-year in which a drawing is necessary such drawing will take place during the last 5 days of May and the last 5 days of November the first of such drawings (if required) to take place during the last 5 days of November 1927 and Bonds so drawn will be redeemed on the next following interest payment date at par together with accrued interest and as from such date interest thereon will cease. The numbers of the Sterling Bonds so drawn will be advertised in such places and in such manner as the Bank shall require. All drawn Bonds presented for payment must have attached thereto all the relative unmatured coupons and talons (if any).

Power is reserved to the (Government of the Republic of Estonia on giving six calendar months' notice by public advertisement to redeem at par with accrued interest the whole or any part of the outstanding Bonds on the 1st day of July 1937 or on any interest payment date thereafter.

The Bonds are the direct obligation of the Republic of Estonia and are secured by a first charge ranking *pari passu* with a like charge securing a loan of £130,000 from Royal Exchange Assurance on the revenues derived from the excise duties on (a) tobacco (b) beer (c) matches (d) cigarette paper yeast wines and liqueurs.

The principal and interest of this Bond are payable :—
(a) Without deduction for any present or future Estonian taxes stamp duties impositions or charges whatsoever; and
(b) Whether in time of peace or war and whether the holder is the subject of a friendly or hostile country.
The Estonian Government will in no case attempt to attach or sequestrate this Bond.

In the event of any interest hereunder not being claimed for a period of 20 years after the due date for payment of the same or in the event of the principal moneys hereunder not being claimed for a period of 30 years after the due date of payment of the same any such principal moneys or interest not so claimed shall revert and belong to the Estonian Government.

A copy of the General Bond securing the Republic of Estonia (Banking and Currency Reform) 7% Loan, 1927 is printed on the back of this Bond.

In witness whereof the Republic of Estonia has caused this Bond to be executed in its name bearing the facsimile signature of its Minister of Finance and to be manually signed by Dr. Oskar Kallas its Minister in London, or other representative, thereunto duly authorised, and the interest coupons bearing the facsimile signature of its Minister of Finance to be hereto annexed.

Dated, London, July 1st, 1927.

REPUBLIC OF ESTONIA.

COUNTERSIGNED FOR VERIFICATION
For and on behalf of
BRITISH, FOREIGN AND COLONIAL CORPORATION LIMITED.

FINANCE MINISTER

ESTONIAN MINISTER IN LONDON.

BRADBURY WILKINSON & CO LD ENGRAVERS NEW MALDEN SURREY ENGLAND

As a counterclaim Britain sought compensation for owners of bonds issued and defaulted by the Baltic States. The result, in 1969, was a settlement whereby of the £5.7 million of gold, £500,000 was used to buy consumer goods for sending to the USSR, and the balance was paid out to holders of the bonds. A story branded at the time as 'squalid'. The bonds redeemed in this way were as follows:

Republic of Estonia	7%	1927
City of Riga	4½%	1913
City of Vilna	5%	1912 and 1931
Wolmar Railway	4½%	1910

Inevitably, not all bonds were handed in, and those remaining are some of the rarest in existence.

CONCLUSION

To say that the number of Russian bonds existing is limitless would be an exaggeration, but it is certainly true to say that this theme of scripophily is by far and away the largest. Despite the length of this chapter, very little mention has been made of the State Loans, an area which lends itself to considerable future research, and this sector will, no doubt, warrant a book to itself as the hobby develops.

The collector choosing Russia as a theme should identify a particular area of interest. Both railways and cities provide excellent collecting themes and these will be made even more so with the forthcoming publication of detailed reference books.

A SAMPLE LISTING OF RUSSIAN BONDS

The following gives an indication of the quality and types of Russian bonds available to the collector. The reference numbers relating to railway bonds are from the Drumm & Henseler catalogue. City bonds have been listed on page 96.

STATE ISSUES

1822 Rothschild Annuity

Issued in 4 denominations (£111, £148, £518, £1,036). Printed on weak paper in black/white with double headed eagle. Total issue £3,661,335. Higher denominations scarce.

1859 3% Imperial Russian Loan

Total amount: £1,621,400. Very few of the £1,000 bonds exist, and forecasts of less than 500 of the £100 have been made. The £100 denomination is printed in black/white. Text in English one side, Russian on reverse.

1906 5% State Loan

Issued in 3 denominations (Frs. 500, Frs. 2,500, Frs. 5,000). 450 series each of varying quality of bonds. Total issue Frs. 250,000,000 of which 99% still outstanding.

1909 4½% State Loan

Issued in 3 denominations as above but with 280 series. Total issue: Frs. 4,400,000,000 which is all outstanding.

BANKS

Imperial Land Mortgage Bank of the Nobility

Various issues from 1897. Total amount still outstanding £87,079,396. Lower denominations very common.

Peasants Land Bank

Various issues and denominations. Total outstanding £10,587,500.

RAILWAYS

1913 4½% Armavir-Tuapse

Cat. No.	Description	Den.	No. issued
SU E 1004 a	Brown/Black	£20	10,001
SU E 1004 b	Blue/Black	£100	7,222
SU E 1004 c	Red/Black	£500	2,600

Loan £2,222,220, Outstanding £2,213,000.

1889 4% Orel-Griasi
Series B

SU E 1098 a	Blue/Black	500 RM	32,448
SU E 1098 b	Red/Black	1,000 RM	18,071
SU E 1098 c	Grey/Black	2,000 RM	7,911

Loan 50,117,000 RM.

1899 4% Moscow-Vindava-Rybinsk

Cat. No.	Description	Den.	No. issued
SU E 1083 a	Brown/Black	£20	3,750
SU E 1083 b	Blue/Black	£100	20,000
SU E 1083 c	Red/Black	£500	1,000
SU E 1083 d	Lilac/Black	£1,000	400

Loan £2,975,000, Outstanding £2,576,000.

1911 4½% Black Sea-Kuban

SU E 1121 a	Orange/Black	£20	28,278
SU E 1121 b	Blue/Black	£100	11,482
SU E 1121 c	Green/Black	£500	400

Loan £1,913,760, Outstanding £1,911,260.

1881 3% Great Russian
3rd Issue

SU E 1021 a	Green/Black	125 Rbl	55,176
SU E 1021 b	Grey/Pink	625 Rbl	10,000

Loan 13,147,000 Gold Rbl, Outstanding 9,539,623 Gold Rbl.

1912 4¼% Kahetian Railway

SU E 1029 a	Brown/Black	£20	20,000
SU E 1029 b	Blue/Black	£100	8,500
SU E 1029 c	Red/Black	£500	300

Loan £1,400,000, Outstanding £1,396,240.

1910 4½% Kokand-Namangan

SU E 1031 a	Brown/Black	£20	6,105
SU E 1031 b	Blue/Black	£100	2,400
SU E 1031 c	Red/Black	£500	80

Loan £402,100, Outstanding £399,840.

1888 4% Kursk-Kharkov-Azov
Series A

SU E 1032 a	Green/Black	600 RM	21,221
SU E 1032 b	Brown/Black	£100	12,087
SU E 1032 c	(max. 81 remain)	£500	111
SU E 1032 d		£1,000	23

Loan £1,287,200, Outstanding £1,056,800.

SOUTH AFRICA

Of all the country themes discussed, South Africa is perhaps the most interesting to the scripophilist. Its commercial history since the 1860s has revolved around mineral resources, particularly gold and diamonds. The share certificates issued to finance development of these minerals clearly reflect the excitement and volatility of an economy based on commodities.

Should such a piece exist, the earliest share certificate relating to South Africa would be one from the Dutch East India Co. (founded in 1602), for it was this company which first annexed, occupied and developed the Cape. But such history is too ancient for the purposes of this book and we must concentrate on the period since 1800, when companies first began to be formed in large numbers.

The first company to be formed and registered in South Africa in 1800 was the 'African Theatre'; initially its profits were simply passed to charity, but by 1821, to the shareholders. Despite the establishment of the Cape Town Commercial Exchange in 1817, it was not until the 1830s that the commercial world really began to move. The first bank was formed in 1831 (Cape of Good Hope Savings Bank) and a variety of other companies sprang up around that period, for example:

The Cape of Good Hope Steam Navigation Co. (1836)	2,000 shares
The Cape of Good Hope Bank (1837)	1,500 shares
Cape Marine Assurance Co. (1838)	1,500 shares

By this time Britain had taken over the Colony which had resulted in the freeing of all slaves. As these were valued at £3 million, a fifty per cent compensation to owners was seen as inadequate and was a major contributory reason for the 'Great Trek' with Boers marching north to found the new lands of the Orange Free State, and the Transvaal.

Although the compensation was believed too small, it did represent a substantial injection of money into the economy thus encouraging commercial development and the discovery of copper in the 1850s was an ideal catalyst. Amongst those many companies formed to mine copper in Namarqualand were:

The South African Mining Co.	2,000 shares of £10 each
The Orange River Mining Co.	1,000 shares of £25 each
The New Burra-Burra Mining Co.	5,000 shares of £50 each
Eagle Mining Co.	10,000 shares of £10 each
The Alliance Mining Co.	5,000 shares of £10 each

But reserves were inadequate and the boom soon collapsed. This pattern of boom and crash was to be followed many times in years to come.

As the copper trend waned, many new companies were formed, the largest of which was the Cape Town Railway & Dock Co. which was capitalized at £600,000 and built the original line to Wellington.

Commercial progress was not limited to Cape Colony and indeed the first railway in South Africa was the Natal Railway Co. which was opened in 1860 and ran between Durban and the Point. The Orange Free State developed rather more slowly with the most significant company being the Bloemfontein Bank, which was later absorbed by the National Bank of the Orange Free State.

Of all the areas to benefit most from mineral discoveries, the Transvaal was, of course, the greatest.

DIAMONDS AND GOLD

The early diamond exploration companies were little more than syndicates of individuals, but by 1869 more formal organizations were materializing. Of these, the Perseverance Co. and the Spes Bona Co. are perhaps the better known. The earliest flotation was of the Hope Town Diamond Co., later taken over by the London-registered London and South Africa Exploration Co. (1870). This latter company acquired the Bullfontein and Dorstfontein areas adjoining Kimberley and was in turn acquired by De Beers in 1899. De Beers itself was formed in 1871.

Fearing that the Zulus were about to overrun the Boer states in 1877, the British annexed Transvaal and eventually beat the Zulus into submission two years later. Unfortunately Britain was slow to hand back the

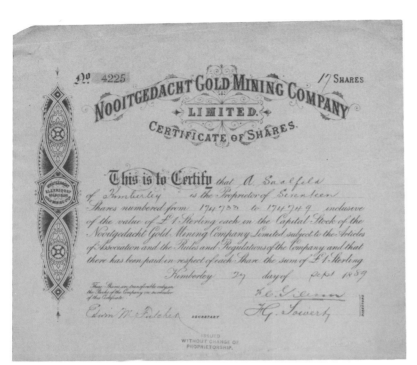

Nooitgedacht Gold Mining Co. Ltd, a Kimberley registered share of 1889.

republics, so prompting Paul Kruger to lead a successful rebellion in 1880 reasserting the independence of the Boer territories. This date coincided with the formation of Kimberley's first stock exchange (the second followed one year later) and the great diamond boom had begun in earnest.

Numerous companies were formed with the total nominal capital invested rising from £2½ million to £8 million within six months. Seventy-one companies were formed, of which thirteen belonged to De Beers. But as with copper, the boom was short-lived and by mid-1881 the crash had set in commemorated by the auctioning off of one of the stock exchanges. By 1888 most diamond companies had been amalgamated into De Beers.

Following the first diamond crash, it was not until 1885 that a major recovery began, this time initiated by the completion of a railway line to the diamond fields, but more significantly influenced by the discovery of gold at Witwatersrand in 1886. Amongst the early gold exploration companies floated at Kimberley were:

> Roodepoort Gold Mining Co. Ltd
> The Alpine Gold Mining Co.
> The Evelyn Gold Mining Co.
> Tati Concessions Mining & Exploration Co.
> Nooitgedacht Gold Mining Co. Ltd

Early gold deposits were so deeply entrenched that mining was difficult and costly. As a result, it was primarily the English who could afford it, particularly those, such as Cecil Rhodes, who had already built up their fortunes from diamond mining.

Several local stock exchanges were set up and in 1889 South Africa had more stockbroking firms per head of population than anywhere else in the world. 750 broking firms served a total (white) population of only half a million. During the gold boom years of 1888–9, the newspapers published editions every hour but, as before, the crash came. This time, it was relatively short-lived and the formation of Rand Mines Ltd in 1893 was a sign for renewed optimism.

THE BOER WAR AND AFTER

War was declared on Britain in 1899 and following many prolonged and bloody encounters was lost by 1902. But it was not until 1910 that the various states of the Transvaal, Orange Free State, Cape Colony and Natal amalgamated to form the Union of South Africa under the premiership of Louis Botha.

A share certificate of the Twyfelhoek Diamond Mine registered in Kimberley in 1889 with two Cape of Good Hope revenue stamps.

The Johannesburg stock exchange was inaugurated in 1904 and in 1917 Ernest Oppenheimer formed the Anglo American Corporation of South Africa. At the time of the Union, there were 7,570 miles of railway track in the country mostly state owned, but composed of three quite different systems: The Central South African Railways, The Cape Government Railways, and The Natal Government Railways. It was not until 1916 that agreement could be reached on a merger.

Even through the early part of this century, the process of boom/crash/boom continued with the last such major event being the platinum boom of 1925.

CONCLUSION

The history of South Africa is closely interwoven with the discovery of precious minerals and their commercial development. The share certificates of the period reflect this process extremely well and provide a compact theme for anyone seeking a link with mining industries. Despite the large number of companies formed over the years (particularly between 1870–95) individual capitalization was often low, and obtaining a fine collection of South African material can be a difficult task.

A SAMPLE LISTING OF SOUTH AFRICAN MATERIAL

Aurora West United Gold Mining Co. Ltd
Green/White. Share certificate. Dated c. 1920.
Company registered under laws of the Transvaal.

Consort Reef Gold Mining Co. Ltd
Blue/White. Share certificate. Dated c. 1890.
Registered at Barberton, South African Republic.
Capital of Company £25,000.

The Du Preez Gold Mining & Estate Co. Ltd
Black/White. Share. Dated c. 1889. Registered at Johannesburg. Capital £300,000.

Free State Mines Ltd
Orange/White. Share. Dated 1895.
Registered Cape of Good Hope. Capital £150,000.
With revenue stamp.

The Heidelberg Gold Mining Co.
Black/White with red overstamp. Dated 1889.
Registered Cape of Good Hope.

Nooitgedacht Gold Mining Co. Ltd
Black/White. Share. Dated 1889. Registered Kimberley.

Twyfelhoek Diamond Mine & Estate Co.
Pale Blue/White with revenue stamps. Dated 1889.
Registered in Cape of Good Hope, issued in Kimberley.

SOUTH AMERICA

Despite representing one-sixth of the world's land mass, South America offers far more economic *possibilities* than economic *history*. Containing only one-twentieth of the world population and enormous mineral reserves ranging from gold to oil, the continent is yet to face its industrial revolution, although many would argue that Brazil, in particular, has taken rapid strides in the last twenty years.

Whereas the European nations drew much of their early wealth from colonialization, South America was very much on the other side of the counter–providing much of that wealth. The continent was basically divided between Spain and Portugal and it was not until the early part of the nineteenth century that the various states achieved independence. Brazil, for example, was not recognized by Portugal as an independent nation until 1825 becoming a republic in 1899.

One of the first prosperous industries to develop in Brazil was that of sugar cane, but gold and diamonds from the area of Minas Gerais were the big crowd pullers, resulting in the growth of Rio de Janeiro as a major port. In the nineteenth century commodities such as rubber and coffee became principally important and these have been supplemented by large reserves of iron ore.

Rare £500 bond of the Argentine Government, 1891.

Above: *Rio de Janeiro – a £20 bond guaranteed by the 'house tax'.*

Right: *A Peruvian certificate of the Compania Territorial de la Bella Union, 1905.*

Opposite: *Aztec-style certificate of the Mexican Petrol Co., 1916.*

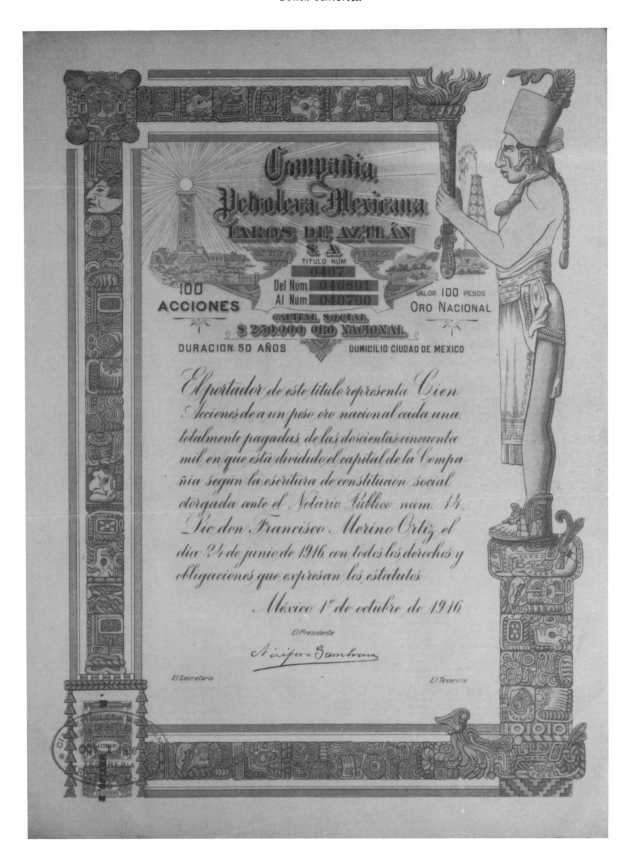

The difficult terrain of the continent made inland development difficult and most of the railways concentrate on short lines to the coastal ports. Only three major areas of extensive railway networks exist; these are the Argentinian Pampas, south eastern Brazil and Central Chile. The railways were of course built and financed by foreigners, and the various share certificates and bonds issued at the time, represent the major collecting segment within this sector. The bonds and debentures in particular, are extremely attractive, often engraved by Waterlow (as in the case of the Brazil Railway Co.) or Bradbury Wilkinson (the Salvador Railway Co.). Many of the original locomotives remain in service, several of which are still wood burners.

Apart from railway material, the South American enthusiast is presented with two other major groups, cities and states, and mining. Of these the former are more readily available ranging from Mexico through Brazil to Chile.

An interesting feature of many of the State guaranteed bonds is their gradual redemption following a period of default. The effect is to reduce the number of outstanding certificates available for collectors, thus increasing their rarity. This policy of redemption is being followed by most of the major States in order to improve their standing in the world of international finance. Brazil and Chile in particular are aiming for a clean bill of health, but Mexico despite its enormous new borrowing on the strength of reputedly vast oil reserves, is showing rather less enthusiasm to pay up on past debts.

South American material for many reasons is highly collectable. It is attractive, relatively scarce and has an 'international flavour' such as that of China and Russia. Much research still needs to be done on the area but with subjects ranging from Macgregor's Poyais, the Panama Canal and construction of the foreign-owned railways, the scripophilist has a fascinating opportunity to acquire a most attractive collection.

A SAMPLE LISTING OF SOUTH AMERICAN MATERIAL

BRAZIL

Brazil Railway Company

4½% First Mortgage 60 year Gold Bonds, 1909; large format; capitalization $6,000,000

£100	Blue/Black
£20	Mauve/Black
Frs 500	Turquoise Green

State of Bahia

5% Gold Bond of 1905: £20 den.; large attractive certificate in Yellow/Orange/Black with vignettes of classical figures. Approx. 88% redeemed. 48,190 issued.

5% Gold Loan of 1913: Vignette of harbour scene with ocean liner. Approx. 88% redeemed; original loan £1 million.

£20 bond	Blue/Black
£100 bond	Green/Black

5% Funding Loan of 1928: Vignette of coat-of-arms ('Per ardua surgo'); £10 bond in Blue/Black.

State of Parana

7% Consolidated bonds; £100 den.; Orange/Black; 7,000 issued, less than 3% outstanding.

Rio de Janeiro

Prefeitura do Districto Federal 5% Loan of 1904, guaranteed by the 'house tax'. Vignette of woman with globe; £20 bond.

COSTA RICA

The Costa Rica Railway Co. Ltd

Attractive bonds with portrait of President Don Bernado Soto Alfaro of Costa Rica, *c.* 1890, all cancelled.
First Mortgage Debenture; £100; 6,550 issued
Second Debenture; £100; 6,000 issued

MEXICO

Mexican National Packing Co. Ltd

6% First and Special Mortgage Gold Bond for $1,000; 1911; 5,000 issued.

Republic Mexicana

1907. Pesos 1,000. Large attractive bond. Vignettes of coat-of-arms, village etc. Brown/Black/White. 740 issued.

OTHER COUNTRIES

Honduras Government Railway Loan

Deferred bearer share in Pink/Black. Signed by 'Honduras Minister in London'. 1867.

Compania Territorial de la Bella Union

Share of 1905. Vignette of miners. Yellow/Brown. Registered in Lima, Peru. Very attractive.

Consolidated Railroads of Cuba

1953. $1,000 bond. Large format, vignettes of train and country scenes. Blue/Black.

La Compania de los Puertos de Cuba (Cuban Ports Co.)

c. 1910. Large share certificate $100. Vignette of allegorical figures with ships in background. Attractive. Grey/White.

Buenos Ayres Lacroze Tramways Co.

1913. £100 Debenture with coupons. Extremely attractive and finely engraved by Waterlow. Vignettes of early trams and founder. Signed by Lacroze. Green/Black.

UNITED STATES OF AMERICA

Much has already been said about historical events of the United States which were reflected in bonds and shares. In future chapters more detail will be devoted to the growth of the railroads, the development of mineral exploration and the background to several famous signatories of the certificates themselves. In view of this, it may seem rather superfluous to devote a major chapter to the United States, but far from it. Our objective is to portray the country as a collecting theme *in toto.* The very nature and variety of the subject has inevitably encroached on other areas, for the bonds and shares of the USA represent such a significant part of the scripophily world that it is essential that we endeavour to pull together the various sub-themes and present an overall picture.

With the exception of the landing of the Mayflower and the eventual Declaration of Independence in 1776 three major events were primarily responsible for shaping the commercial development of the United States, prior to the twentieth century, the first of these was the building of the railroads which began in 1830 and continued for the following seventy years; the second was the discovery and exploitation of minerals, possibly most glamorously portrayed by the California Gold Rush of 1849; and the third was the Civil War of 1861–5. These three features are most amply depicted by the bond and share issues of the time and the pages which follow cover a wide range both in text and illustration.

EARLY COMMERCIAL ACTIVITY

So far as the scripophilist is concerned the earliest known American share certificates date from around 1795. Although there were no doubt several companies formed and operating at that time, the two certificates which most frequently come to light are those of the North American Land Company and the Philadelphia & Lancaster Turnpike Road. Both usually bear the signatures of famous individuals, namely Robert Morris and William Bingham respectively.

A signatory to the American Declaration of Independence, Robert Morris was born in England. Following emigration he became a well known and respected figure of early America. At one time his personal credit exceeded that of the country and he was a close friend of George Washington. This relationship and his standing in the country is evidenced by his portrayal on the Betsy Ross certificate described on page 14. His later involvement in certain land speculation schemes unfortunately led to a period of imprisonment and his eventual death in 1806.

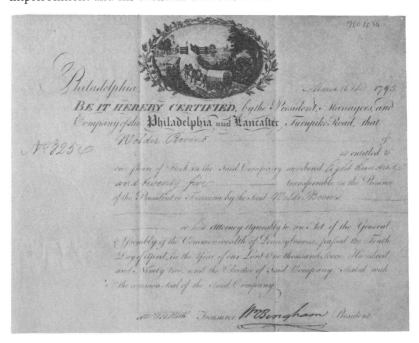

One of the earliest-known American pieces – Philadelphia & Lancaster Turnpike Road Co. dated 1795 and printed on vellum.

The Philadelphia & Lancaster Turnpike Road was the first of its kind in the United States. It was 62 miles long and cost $465,000 to build. The share certificates are possibly the first to carry a vignette and are finely engraved on vellum. William Bingham, the company's president, was also a well-known financier and public figure of Pennsylvania. The certificates usually carry a series of endorsements on the back indicating their progressive ownership. It is interesting to note that many passed through the Biddle family – Nicholas Biddle being the president of the Second Bank of the United States.

IMPROVED COMMUNICATIONS

Following the opening of the first steam railway, the Baltimore and Ohio, in 1830, attention was diverted to this promising means of communication and away from the more traditional horse-drawn vehicles and water transport.

Early development of the railroads is covered in some detail in the later chapter on 'Railways' and the story of Vanderbilt is referred to in the chapter on 'Signatures'. Both the railway certificates themselves and their often famous signatories each make fascinating collecting themes.

One of the most appealing features of these certificates is their attractiveness. Most are engraved on good quality paper and carry vignettes of locos or related scenes. The bonds are usually of specific issue and this is written on the document itself, although some were issued on the basis of being tied to the number of miles of track actually built. Many, such as that of the Blue Ridge Railroad Co. were guaranteed by the State – in this example, the State of Carolina and the City of Charleston, in gold; while others were issued by the State on behalf of a railroad company, such as the $1,000 bonds of 1868 issued by the State of North Carolina to finance the Wilmington Charlotte and Rutherford Railroad Co.

There were reputed to be over 9,000 different US railroad companies formed over the seventy years or so of railway expansion. Many got no further than printing share certificates (which explains the presence of so many unissued pieces) but many others prospered and attracted the attention of most of the financial whiz kids of the time. Not the least of these was Jay Gould, whose signature appears on several company certificates, but most frequently on those of the Missouri Kansas and Texas Railroad Co. In the process of becoming one of the wealthiest men in the country, Gould succeeded in becoming one of the most disliked through his unscrupulous business methods.

The prospective collector of US railway certificates is faced with a wide range of prices and specialist sub-fields. Modern certificates (around 1940) with train vignettes can be picked up for a few pounds, whereas early material, particularly pre-1860 can cost upwards of many hundreds. The collector with an eye to investment is recommended to select pieces from the following categories:

   1 Those bearing famous signatures.
   2 Share certificates dated pre-1860, in reasonable condition.
   3 Bonds (of limited issue) pre-1900.

During the same period as the railways were expanding, express companies also began to develop. These companies carried money, documents or other valuables on behalf of clients, and, as may be gleamed from the story of the American Express Co. (on page 100), played an important part in the overall commercial growth of the United States.

GOLD!

While the railway lines were expanding and moving out towards the west, the California gold rush began in May 1848, only one year after the 'transfer' of the State from Mexican to American ownership.

The impact on the development of the West Coast was enormous. The population grew from 26,000 in 1848 to 115,000 by the end of 1849. About a quarter of the increase were foreigners from Europe, Australia and China and many formed themselves into small companies so as to share both rewards and losses. There are many interesting share certificates of the period, often with low capital and consequently low issues, and the sector makes an interesting collecting field both as a part of the overall framework of the United States and as a separate subject which can easily be expanded to encompass other gold discoveries of the time such as those in Australia and South Africa.

But it was not only gold and other precious metals which were discovered. Coal and iron ore were equally important, albeit not so glamorous. Many certificates, this time from the East Coast, bear witness to these developments and the $100 bonds of the Stafford Meadow Coal Iron City Improvement Co. of 1858 are excellent examples.

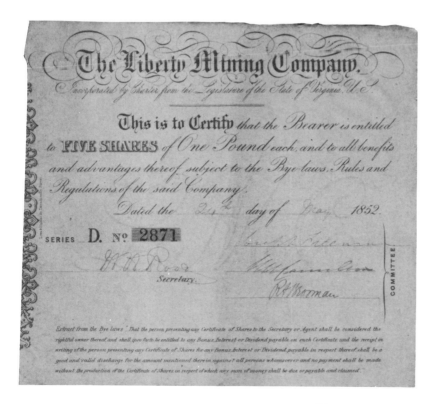

Above: *State of Arkansas $500 bond of 1871.*

Left: *The Liberty Mining Co., an 1852 gold rush certificate.*

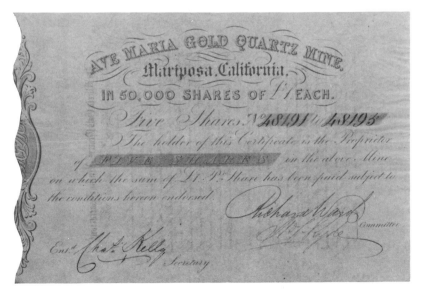

Opposite: *The City of St Petersburg £100 bond of 1914 showing the city coat of arms.*

Above: *The Stafford Meadow Coal Iron City Improvement Co. A $100 bond of 1858 showing a wide variety of vignettes.*

Right: *The Ave Maria Gold Quartz Mine, California – a certificate from the gold rush period.*

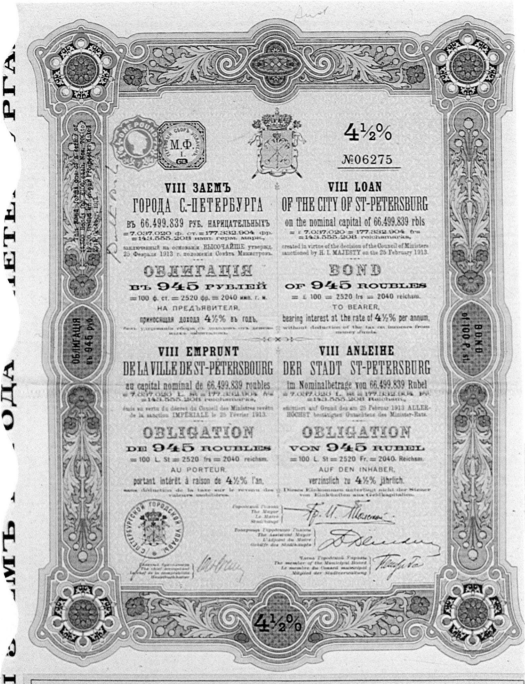

Above: *A Confederate bond of 1863 depicting the George Washington statue.*

Right: *The Marconi Wireless Telegraph Co., 1912.*

Opposite above: *A bearer share in the Mizrahi Bank, Jerusalem, printed in English and Hebrew.*

Opposite below: *The City of Providence Sewer Loan of 1892. $1,000 bond with a vignette of settlers greeting Indians 'What Cheer'!*

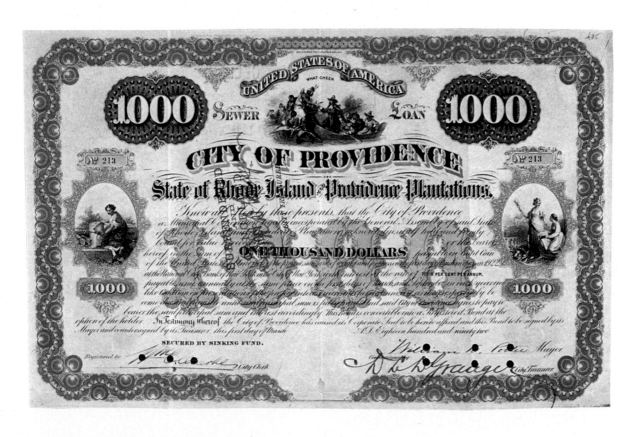

Right: *A 1945 diamond company in the Central African Republic.*

Opposite: *A State of Louisiana $1,000 cancelled bond of 1892.*

THE CIVIL WAR

Mention has already been made of the Confederate Bonds issued to finance the Civil War of 1861–5. In an earlier chapter attention was drawn to the historical significance of these documents which without doubt makes them extremely worth while collecting. Here we are more concerned with the intrinsic nature of the bonds themselves – how they were printed, how many were issued and where they are now.

First the printing. Lack of funds and time meant that little attention was paid to the quality of printing of both banknotes and bonds issued by the Confederacy. As a result counterfeiting was prevalent, but it would appear that this was concentrated on the banknote side rather than the bonds which were a little better controlled. The poor quality of paper used, however, has resulted in the gradual disintegration of a great many certificates. As many as ten different companies were used to print the bonds.

The number of bonds issued has been determined by reference to the original Acts of Congress and the results have been catalogued (see bibliography). There are approximately 170 different bond types and a further ninety or so variations. Thus it is feasible to complete a collection, but certainly not easy, due to the relatively small issues of certain bonds (several, less than 500). Although the amount of money raised in total by the Confederates was vast, this is not quite the same as saying that the number of pieces of paper was equally vast. Most of the bonds are high denominations $500 or $1,000 or more, thus considerably limiting the quantities issued.

To answer the question of where they are now, it is first necessary to realize that the vast majority of the bonds were sold in Europe, particularly Britain and France, to those businessmen keen to maintain a steady flow of cotton through the flourishing mills of the period. With the loss of the war and the consequent default, a council was established in England with the objective of recovering all or some of the debt. Bondholders were invited to place their bonds with the council in return for 'scrip certificates' proving ownership and indicating that the bonds were being held by the National Safe Deposit Company Limited. Over the years, the deposited bonds were moved on several occasions. They are now in the vaults of Coutts Bank in London who are faced with the legal dilemma of whether they are the legal owners or not, and if not, who is? Not all are in this one location and many change hands through dealers and auctions.

CONCLUSION

It is quite simply impossible to cover a subject as widespread as the United States in a single chapter, but hopefully the references and pointers given, will provide the collector with some feeling for the theme.

Jefferson Davis and a view of Richmond depicted on a $1,000 bond of 1863.

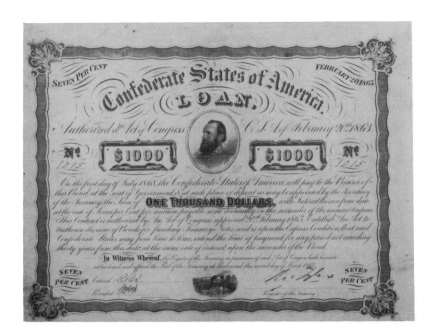

$1,000 Confederate bond of 1863 portraying General 'Stonewall' Jackson.

A SAMPLE LISTING OF US MATERIAL

RAILROADS

(A.B.N.C. = American Bank Note Company)

Baltimore & Ohio Railroad Company

1893 96 $100 shares. Vignette of very early train. Olive & White. A.B.N.C.

Belt Railroad & Stock Yard Co.

$50 shares. Preferred stock 1950s. Vignette of train in station; Black on White.

Boston, Clinton & Fitchburg Railroad Co.

1872–75. Woman leaning on shield depicting Indian. Train over bridge, 2 sailing ships. Share certificates (issued). Black on White.

Boston, Clinton, Fitchburg & New Bedford Railroad Co.

18__. Bottom centre shield depicting Indian; sailing boat. A.B.N.C. Unissued. Black on White.

Boston Elevated Railway Co.

Vignette of electric train on overhead system:
   Preferred shares; Green & Black; 1926
   Second preferred shares; Blue/Black/White; 1927–29
   $100 shares; Maroon/Black/White; A.B.N.C.; 1913

Boston Hartford & Erie Railway Co.

$1,000 bond dated 1863. Attractive vignettes on bond & coupons. Green/Black/Orange.

Chicago & Alton

1899 $1,000 bonds; Green/Black; vignette of train; issued.

Chicago, Burlington & Kansas City

188_. Train with goods carriages; $100 shares; unissued; Black on White.

Chicago, Burlington & Northern

188_. Green/Black certificate; train in oval frame supported by mythical beasts. A.B.N.C. Unissued.

Chicago, Burlington and Quincy Railroad Company

Black & White with train; $100 shares; 1884; A.B.N.C.
Brown & White with train; $100 shares; 1884.
Black & White; rural scene with train; $100 share dated 25 April 1873.

Chicago & Eastern, Illinois

Vignette of train with men working on line; A.B.N.C.
   c. 1920 Common $100 shares; Orange; unissued
   c. 1920 Preferred $100 shares; Brown unissued
   c. 1920 Less than $100 shares; Green; unissued

Chicago & Eastern Illinois

Vignette of train standing at station and train pulling goods wagons; attractive format:
   c. 1900; less than $100 shares; common stock; Olive and White
   1897; 100 common shares; Green/Black
Train in siding:
   1905; less than $100 preferred shares; Blue/White
   1890s 100 preferred shares; Brown; unissued

Kansas City, Mexico and Orient Railway Co.

1911. Preferred stock trust certificate; Orange & Black with vignette of train in countryside.

Kentucky & Great Eastern Railway Co.

1872. $1,000 bond with all coupons and vignette of Daniel Boone shooting Indians; unissued.

Missouri Kansas & Texas Railway Co.

Vignette of train in goods yard (circular building).
Common stock; Red, White & Black; c. 1900
Common stock; 10 shares; Brown, White & Black;
c. 1890
100 shares common; Green, White & Black; c. 1900

The Rock Island Co.

c. 1919; common stock; Brown & Black with vignette of
station scene.

St Lawrence & Adirondack

19__. Train, paddle steamer; Red & White; $100 share;
unissued.

Tarkio Valley Railroad Co.

18__. Sepia coloured certificate with vignette of train and
ship; unissued.

Tennessee North Eastern

1909. 5% First Mortgage Bond; English & French text;
$100.

CONFEDERATE BONDS

(Catalogue numbers relate to Criswell Catalogue)

Catalogue No.	Den.	No. Issued	Identification
3	$500	200	John C. Calhoun 1782–1850
	(Montgomery)		U.S. Vice President 1824–1832
5	$50	7,835	Commerce & Agriculture (thick paper)
6	$100	7,950 (all types)	Commerce & Agriculture (thick paper)
6A	$50		As above, but thin fibre paper
7	$500	5,250	White with green arabic numerals
8	$1,000	7,071	As above
12	$500	319	Commerce & train at centre. Indian warrior left, Indian Princess on right
19	$50	998	General Pierre Gustave Toutant de Beauregard
20	$50	3,614	Thomas Bragg
27	$100	628	George Washington
29	$100	8,884	Senator R. M. T. Hunter; dog & chest at base
31	$100	916	J. P. Benjamin (Confederate Secretary of State)
32	$100	2,294	Thomas Bragg. Border of 3 female figures
34	$100	E.2,000	S. R. Mallory (Confederate Secretary of the Navy)
36	$100	1,094	J. H. Reagan (Postmaster General), surrounded by 3 female figures
41	$100	1,454	General Beauregard
43	$100 (both types)	1,769	J. P. Benjamin. Litho by 'B. Duncan, Columbia, S.C.'
43A	$100	(both types)	As above, but no engraver's name
44	$100	1,615	Thomas Bragg
45	$100	1,399	Senator R. M. T. Hunter
46	$100	1,798	Thomas Bragg
47	£100	1,901	Senator R. M. T. Hunter
48	$100	2,000	Edward C. Elmore, dog & chest at base
62	$500	1,388	J. H. Reagan (Postmaster General)
63	$500	1,397	S. R. Mallory, surrounded by 3 female figures
64	$500	1,408	George W. Randolph (Secretary of War); surrounded by 3 female figures
66	$500	1,650	T. H. Watts, surrounded by 3 female figures
68	$500	1,831	George W. Randolph (Secretary of War)
70	$500	1,971	Alexander Stephens (elected 1st Vice President, Confederate States 1861)

COMPANIES

Acacia Gold Mining Co.

Certificate for 1,000 shares; vignette of acacia blossom;
White/Gold/Green; c. 1899.
As above, but Black/White; c. 1900.

Algoma Bondholders Joint Committee

Trust certificate; 1917

Alexander Young Co. Distillers Ltd

Vignette of factory; Black/White; unissued 188__.

Ave Maria Gold Quartz Mine

Bearer share certificate for 5 shares; 1851.

American Oak Leather

1899; vignette of factory; $100 shares.

Black Diamond Copper Mining Co.

Vignettes of miners; Green/Black with Green seal; share
certificate; c. 1900.

Brokers Gold Mining Co.

Vignette of miners at work; Green & Black with Gold seal;
unissued; c. 1880.

The Liberty Mining Co.

Bearer certificate of 1852.

Marconi Wireless Telegraph Co.

Olive Green & Black; vignette of world & telegraph pylons;
c. 1920.

Maryland Brewing Co.

Coat-of-arms; British revenue stamp; all shares made out to
William Drinkwater Freeth! 1899.
   Common stock; Black & White
   Preferred stock; Brown & White

The Nouveau Monde Company

For 'Working Gold Mines in California'. Bearer certificate in
French & English. c. 1850.

Patti Rosa Gold Mining Co., Colorado

189_. Unissued certificate in Black/Gold with vignette of
miners working.

Pithole & Kanawha Oil Co.

186_. Capital $500,000; heraldic vignette; Black & White;
$2.50 shares; unissued.

BANKS

Bank of Charleston, South Carolina

c. 1870; woman standing; ball of cotton & heraldic vignette.

Briggs National Bank of Clyde

1898; vignettes of country scene and sailing ship.

First National Bank of Cooperstown

1882; share certificate in Black & White with vignette.

Second National Bank of Boston

Certificate with 3 vignettes; 1927; A.B.N.C.

Waverley Co-Operative Bank (Massachusetts)

1952; vignettes of house; Green & White.

STATES

State of Georgia

$500 bond with coupons, signed by Governor Joseph
Brown, 1862; Black/White with vignettes of state seal, docks
and battle scene (Criswell 61A).

State of Louisiana

Very attractive certificate with vignettes of castle &
allegorical figures, c. 1900:
   $100; Brown/Black
   $500; Orange/Black
   $1,000; Green/Black

Republic of Texas

$100 bond issued in 1841; Black/White with vignettes of
cow, paddle boat etc. (40A).

$500 bond as above, but vignettes of Indian and farm scene
(40B).

$500 bond, 1840; vignettes of sailor and allegorical figures;
Series A (40F).

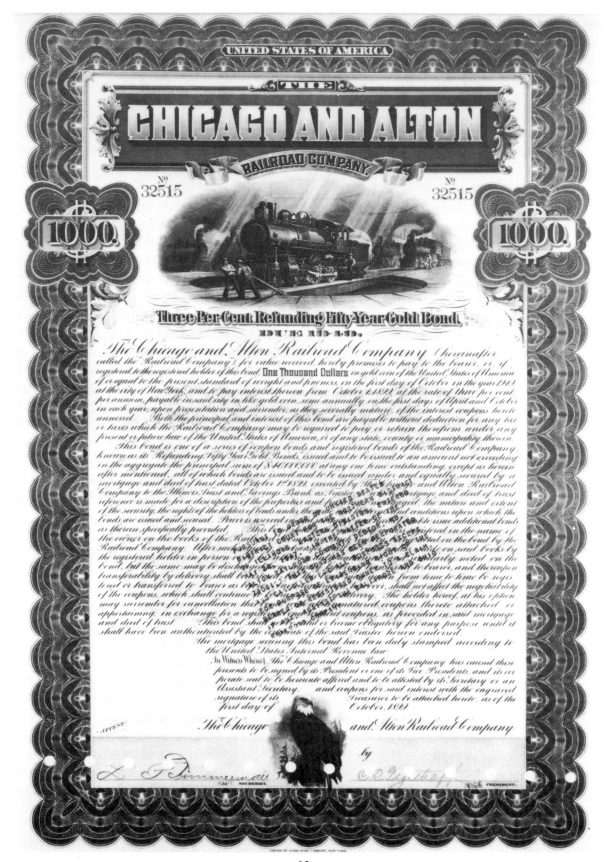

RAILWAYS

What is it about railways that fascinates so many people? Is it the gleaming brass fittings, the clouds of smoke or the endless lengths of track? All presumably play their part but one thing is certain, of all the inventions since the industrial revolution, none matched the railway for public enthusiasm both at birth and during life.

This book is about bonds and shares not railways, a subject on which much has already been written, but our paths cross as the building of railways needed financing – a lot of financing, and it is primarily this aspect with which we are concerned.

EARLY DAYS

The earliest 'railway' (that is to say, a vehicle drawn by a horse along wooden rails) is believed to have been built in 1603 at Wollaton, England. Many such tracks followed but it was not until around 1780 that wooden rails were replaced by cast iron. By 1810 there was already 300 miles of track in Britain. The development was encouraged by the increasing cost of transport, particularly for minerals – thus most of the lines grew up in the industrial areas, notably the Midlands, the North East and Cornwall.

It was in Cornwall that the idea of steam traction was born. Being the centre of tin mining, stationary steam engines were already in active use, but it was the son of the Dolcoath Mine's manager, Richard Trevithick, who first attempted to introduce the mobile engine. In 1803 he succeeded in driving his steam carriage up the Tottenham Court Road in London much to the amusement, derision and shock of passers-by. Lack of money and patience caused him to abandon further development work, but others continued, albeit slowly and over the next twenty years only thirty experimental locos were built – all slower than the reliable horse.

1825 saw the opening of the Stockton and Darlington, the first steam-drawn passenger and freight railway in the world. The engine, built by George Stephenson was named 'Locomotion' and was aided on parts of the track by the occasional horse. The line soon began to make money, with dividends rising from $2\frac{1}{2}\%$ in 1826 to 8% in 1832 and to 15% in 1839.

Investors were encouraged, but it was the even greater success of the Liverpool and Manchester Railway which really sparked the 'mania' (the name given to such investment enthusiasms). The directors of the Liverpool and Manchester offered a prize of £500 to the designer of a loco which had to be less than 6 tons, able to pull a load three times its own weight and travel at a minimum speed of 10 mph. The winner was, of

Opposite: *The Chicago & Alton Railroad Co. $1,000 bond showing a scene of Jesse James' last hold-up in 1881.*

Left: *Blaydon, Gateshead & Hebburn Railway, an extremely early certificate of an industrial railway company. Printed on vellum and dated 1835.*

course, Stephenson's 'Rocket' with an incredible top speed of 30 mph. The Liverpool and Manchester was the first wholly mechanical railway being worked entirely by steam traction. From the outset it was a fantastic financial success and regularly paid a 9½% dividend – an appreciably better return than Government securities.

The early British railways were largely financed by the local aristocracy and *nouveau riche* industrialists. Of the 4,233⅓ shares issued for the Liverpool and Manchester, nearly half were taken up by local citizens and one thousand of the remainder by the Marquess of Stafford. Share certificates of the railway dated 1829–30 are printed on vellum and are one of the earliest railway items available. Those of the Stockton and Darlington tend to be preference shares issued in 1859, and as such reflect the decline in railway earnings around that period, which led investors to demand the greater security of preference shares and debentures, as opposed to ordinary common stock.

As the collector may well come across various issue documents of the early British rail companies, it may be helpful to summarize the capital-raising process:

1 A company publishes a prospectus and invites applications.
2 Applicants are sent letters of allotment showing the number of shares allocated and the deposit required.
3 On payment of the deposit a receipt is issued and later exchanged for a scrip certificate.
4 Once Government approval has been obtained by Act of Incorporation, the scrip is exchanged for shares and the investor called upon to pay further instalments up to the full nominal value of the shares.

During the difficult period of 1850–60 when investors were more cautious, other methods of financing were used. One of these was to persuade building contractors to accept mortgage bonds in lieu of payment: a good example was the North Staffordshire Railway which issued £45,000 of bonds to the contractor, Thomas Brassey (who later built the Grand Trunk Railway of Canada) in exchange for construction work.

OVERSEAS DEVELOPMENT

The growth of the steam railway was not limited to the British Isles although it certainly started there and the country was primarily responsible for the building of most overseas networks. Even in 1839 export orders for the British locomotives were so large that a shortage of materials developed. But it was not only the ironmongery which was exported; Welsh coal was specially shipped to stoke the boilers of trains in South America and, more significantly, expertise was sent far and wide, with such notables as Robert Stephenson travelling from Brazil to Russia designing and building the world's great railways.

The table below identifies the first commercial steam railways in the major industrialized countries:

YEAR	COUNTRY	LINE
1825	Great Britain	Stockton & Darlington
1830	USA	Baltimore & Ohio
1832	France	Paris–St Germain
1832	Austria	Budweis–Linz
1835	Germany	Nürnberg–Fürth
1837	Russia	St Petersburg–Pavlovsk
1839	Holland	Amsterdam–Haarlem
1844	Switzerland	Zurich–Basle

The greater number, of course, are in Europe and most of these were centred on the mining areas of those countries. At least three, however, those of France, Germany and Russia, originated as playthings of their countries' rulers.

RUSSIA

Tsar Nicolas I of Russia, impressed by a visit to Britain, granted a concession to a company to build a 24 km railway from St Petersburg to Pavlovsk via the Summer Palace. Two locomotives were ordered, a Stephenson and a Hackworth, and on arrival were promptly baptized by the Greek Orthodox Church. A somewhat bizarre beginning for what is now the largest single railway system in the world. But it is interesting to note that even this small line was profitable generating a 4% dividend in 1839, 7% in 1856.

Left: *1911 Black Sea-Kuban Railway Co., £100 bond.*

Below: *The Great Russian Railway bond of 1861 – 125 silver roubles.*

The first significant line in Russia, however, was not completed until 1848 (Warsaw–Vienna) but after this date progress was swift and the completion of the Moscow–St Petersburg line, later renamed the Nicolas Railway (now the October Railway) set the tone for future development. Many newly-formed railway companies were financed by foreign capital with funds coming from Britain, France, Belgium, Germany and Holland. The amount of money involved, raised through the issue of shares and bonds, was so vast that the debts soon had to be guaranteed by the State in order to reassure foreign investors, but in the end to no avail. Defaulted Russian railway bonds are of such complexity and quantity that they now offer the scripophilist choosing to specialize in this area a fascinating challenge.

THE UNITED STATES OF AMERICA

Seemingly quite independent of the activities in Europe, and shortly before the opening of the Liverpool and Manchester Railway, the United States entered the field.

The Baltimore and Ohio Railway Co. was incorporated in 1827. Charles Carroll, a director of the company (and at the time the sole surviving signatory of the Declaration of Independence) ceremoniously began its building, turning the first spade of earth in 1828. The train, named 'Tom Thumb', was designed and built by Peter Cooper from an assortment of scrap metal using gun barrels for boiler tubes. The first stretch of the line from Baltimore to Ellicotts Mills was opened in January 1830 and in August a race was arranged between train and horse. Horse won, but only just.

From that time on, the race to open up new lines began but it was not until the 1850s that progress was really made. The difficult terrain and varied weather conditions of the USA emphasized the inadequacies and unreliability of the early locos. The Chicago and Rock Island RR was the first to reach the Mississippi in 1854, closely followed by the Illinois Central and the Chicago and Alton. Despite often violent objections by the rivermen, the river was finally bridged in 1856.

The Civil War of 1861 spurred Lincoln into the joining of east and west and so preventing any possible breakaway by the West Coast states. The Central Pacific RR of California was incorporated in 1861 and the following year saw the launch of the Union Pacific RR. But it was not until May 1869 that the two great lines met at Promontory, Utah – now a famous tourist attraction.

The Baltimore & Ohio Railroad Co. A certificate of 1892 showing the 'Tom Thumb' train travelling along the first American railway.

Left: *The Kentucky & Great Eastern Railway – a $1,000 bond of 1872 showing Daniel Boone shooting Indians.*

Below: *A certificate for ten shares in The Rock Island Co. of New Jersey. Printed by the American Bank Note Company of New York.*

At one stage there were in excess of 9,000 different railroad companies operating in the United States. Many were eventually merged into groups controlled by railway kings such as Gould, Vanderbilt and Drew. The collector of bonds and shares of these companies is thus faced with a wide variety of material. Unlike Russian bonds, those of the United States invariably carry attractive vignettes of the trains or railway scenes; they are finely engraved and often of limited issue, although the issue of some was tied to the length of track built. Many early share certificates bear interesting signatures (see page 104).

CHINA

Mention has already been made of the railway bonds of China on page 29, but it may be interesting to expand a little on the early beginning of steam in that vast and exotic country, particularly as many of the original steam locos continue to run on those same unpaid-for tracks.

It was not until 1876 that the Chinese risked this new mode of transport and even then, the ten-mile railway from Shanghai to Woosung, designed and built by British engineers, was viewed with constant suspicion – a suspicion finally 'confirmed' by the death of a Chinaman run down by the 'smoking dragon'. As a result, the Government took over the railway, ripped it up and dumped it in Formosa.

Five years later, C. W. Kinder surreptitiously constructed a track at Kaiping to transport coal. The engine was locally made and named 'The Rocket of China'. But even that nomenclature could not save it from the government inspector who promptly had it buried. It was later exhumed and put back into service.

Although during the latter part of the 1880s China built a few short lines, within ten years it was once again issuing concessions to foreigners. One of the most important of these was the building of the Chinese Eastern Railway by the Russians in 1897. The table below gives some idea of the split between local and foreign financing:

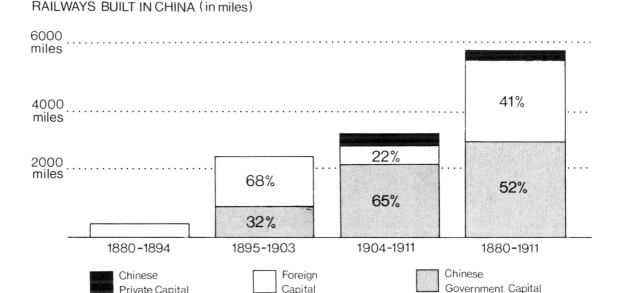

RAILWAYS BUILT IN CHINA (in miles)

The railway system progressed and by about 1907 it was possible to travel from London to the Far East, via the Trans-Siberian and the Chinese Eastern Railways, in a little over two weeks. Following the 1911 revolution and the removal of the Emperor, the Chinese Government endeavoured to bring all the railways under their control. Foreign funds were still used, but the railways were constructed and managed by Chinese with the assistance of foreign technicians. From around 1925, the railways fell completely under Chinese jurisdiction, but despite this, Europe continued to be the main source of finance as evidenced by the defaulted bonds. Completing a collection of Chinese railway bonds is an achievable objective and not as daunting a task as obtaining all US or Russian paper; it can, however, be expensive as many are of low issue and extremely rare.

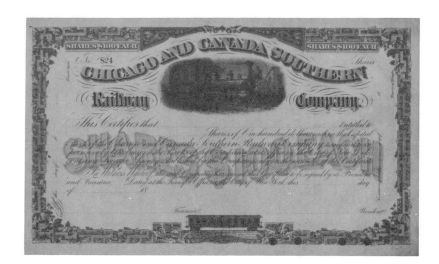

The Chicago & Canada Southern – unissued share.

SOUTH AMERICA

The somewhat chaotic nature of South American railways stems from their haphazard development. Most were built relatively recently and usually for reasons of exploitation rather than local communication. They were almost entirely built and financed by foreign investors of such diversity that the result has been considerable incompatibility of equipment. The bonds issued to finance their construction are usually extremely attractive and finely engraved by Waterlow or Bradbury Wilkinson.

Although many passed through a period of default, most of the countries are now correcting the position and gradually redeeming their outstanding debts. This has the inevitable result of increasing the rarity of those remaining.

SOUTH AFRICA

Prior to the discovery of diamonds in 1869 and gold in 1886, there was little need or interest in railways in South Africa. But with the changed economy the race to develop communications became frantic. Cecil Rhodes succeeded in extending the Cape Government Railway northward from Kimberley and in 1892 the first train reached Johannesburg. Following the Boer War and the formation of the Union in 1910 considerable efforts were made to consolidate the various lines and in 1916, the three major systems of the Central South African Railways, the Cape Government Railways, and the Natal Government Railways, merged.

CONCLUSION

From this relatively brief foray into the world of steam, the collector will have gathered some idea of the vastness of the field even within bonds and shares. It would be an extravagant objective to aim to collect all railway material, and for this reason it is recommended that collectors segment the overall theme, possibly choosing a particular country or period. Whatever your choice, this theme offers enormous scope.

CITIES

The number of cities which issued bonds and subsequently defaulted on their repayment is surprisingly small, and well short of the vast number of railway companies. The most prolific country was, of course, Russia, and this will be dealt with in more detail shortly. Other significant sources were Germany and Mexico, but in relatively recent years, there have been a number of issues by cities of the United States. These latter bonds were not defaulted (although New York came close recently), and are only cancelled after repayment.

City bonds were issued to finance such typical municipal projects as the building of schools and hospitals, the laying of sewers, the electrification of street lighting and the construction of local roads. Such purposes were rarely too specifically stated, in order to give the city fathers maximum flexibility as to how the money was eventually used.

Right: 1914 City of Kiev £100 bond – it shows the city coat of arms. 3,180 were issued.

Opposite: The City of Bergen £100 bond – fully repaid, and one of only a few still existing.

RUSSIAN CITIES

Between the period of 1891–1915, twenty-eight Russian cities raised loans, some such as Moscow had several issues so that the total number exceeded one hundred. On the basis of an average three denominations per issue, this presents the collector with a target of around 300 pieces; not a large figure in itself, but nevertheless a very difficult one to achieve for two main reasons. One, some issues were extremely small (e.g. City of Nicolaiev 2nd issue which in total amounted to only £41,620) and two, several bonds were issued internally only, that is to say, they were generally not available outside Russia and thus have been largely destroyed: an example is the City of Poti 5% loan of 1896.

The purpose of the loan is often indicated on the back of the bonds themselves and can make interesting reading. The 1912 City of Nicolaiev issues, for example, were issued, amongst other things, for the 'purchase of the enterprise of the Belgian Company Ltd of the existing tramways of Nicolaiev with horse traction', and perhaps more intriguingly 'for increasing the floating means of the municipal pawnbrokery'!

Most of the foreign-issued bonds bear facsimile signatures of the mayor, two members of the municipal authority and the book-keeper; the latter signature is usually original, as he no doubt had to carry the can if things went wrong. These bonds were quoted on most of the major European stock exchanges (Paris, Berlin, London, Amsterdam and Brussels) and are often written in four languages.

Many of the original Russian city names have changed over the years and it can be an interesting task locating them on a map. In view of the fairly small populations at the turn of the century it is a little difficult to understand what happened to all the money raised. In 1897 populations were as follows:

St Petersburg	1,267,023
Moscow	988,610
Kiev	248,750
Nicolaiev	92,060

Apart from the interesting economic features of the bonds, collectors will also find the designs particularly appealing. Most bear the coat of arms of the city and have attractive intricate border designs. As a collecting theme which combines history, rarity and attractiveness, Russian Cities make an ideal topic.

Right: *The Transcaucasian Railway – an 1882 bond for 125 roubles.*

Opposite: *Ten shares in the Russian Tobacco Company issued in 1912 and engraved by Waterlow.*

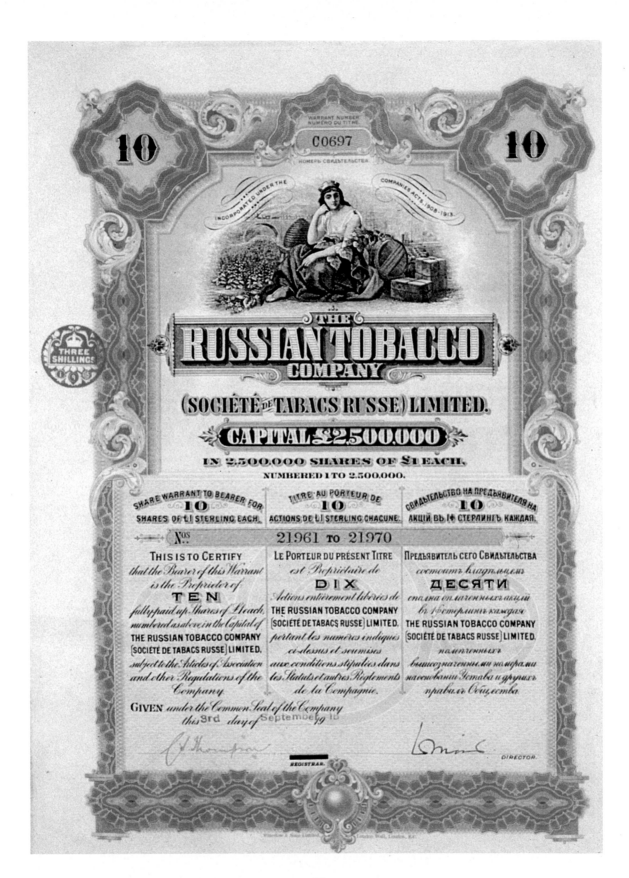

Opposite: *The Oriental Shipping Co. of Greece, a superb example of contemporary art styles at work on scrip.*

Left: *The City of Odessa 100 rouble bond of 1902.*

OTHER CITIES

Several city issues outside Russia have been listed in the summary catalogue following. Those of Germany (particularly City of Dresden) and Shanghai, are perhaps the most interesting, but there remains much research to be done in the field and the collector choosing the theme has excellent opportunities to develop the subject further.

SAMPLE LISTING OF CITY BONDS

RUSSIA

1910 5% City of Baku

Den.	Description	No. Issued
£20	Brown	71,432
£100	Light & Dark Blue	12,860
£500	Red	285

Proposed loan of £2,857,140; Issued £2,843,060; Outstanding £2,773,860.

1914 5% City of Kiev

£20	Beige/Dark Green	5,300
£100	Pink/Dark Green	3,180
£500	Light & Dark Green	212

22nd Loan £665,660; Issued £530,000; Outstanding £522,520.

1908 5% City of Moscow

£20	Orange/Brown	59,778
£100	Blue/Lilac	4,940
£500	Red	400

Loan £1,889,560; Outstanding £1,784,560.

1912 4½% City of Moscow

£20	Yellow/Brown	50,001
£100	Light/Dark Green	12,500
£500	Red	1,669
£1,000	—	725

Loan for £3,809,520; Outstanding £3,686,820.

1912 5% City of Nicolaiev

Total loan of £687,820 issued in two tranches:

1st issue: £646,200

£20	Light & Dark Brown	6,475
£100	Light & Dark Blue	3,862
£500	Red	261

2nd issue: £41,620

£20	Light & Dark Brown	401
£100	Light & Dark Blue	266
£500	Red	14

Amount outstanding from both issues: £674,840.

1913 4½% City of Riga

£20	Brown	6,137
£100	Light & Dark Blue	6,000
£500		600
£1,000		300

Loan £1,322,740.
In 1934 40% was redeemed and balance subsequently paid under the provisions of Foreign Compensation (USSR) Order, 1969.

1913 4½% City of St Petersburg

£20	Salmon/Green/Brown	12,500
£100	Blue/Green/Rust	14,500
£500	Red/Green	200
£1,000	Greens/Pink	500

8th Loan of £7,037,020.

GERMANY

City of Dresden 5% 1927

Den.	Description	No. Issued
£100	Light/Dark Green	3,700
£500	Red	360
£1,000		50

Total Loan £600,000 of which £299,400 remains outstanding.

Free State of Saxony 6% 1927

£20	Orange/Black with vignette.	2,000
£100		5,350
£500		350

Total Loan £750,000 of which £527,780 remains outstanding.

CHINA

Shanghai Municipal Council

5% loan bond for $1,000	Red/Black	1934

Engraved by Waterlow.

Shanghai Municipal Council

5% loan bond for $500	Blue/Black	1937

UNITED STATES

City of Providence

$1,000 Water Refunding Loan	Blue/Black	c. 1900
$1,000 Sewer Loan	Orange/Black	c. 1893
$1,000 Highway Loan	Brown/Black	c. 1894

All above with vignette of settlers meeting Indians 'What cheer'.

City of Jersey City

$1,000 School Bond	Green/Black	c. 1921

Facsimile signature of Mayor—'Boss' Hagen, Gangster.

OTHER COUNTRIES

City of Bergen

$100 Vignette of Harbour	Red/Black	1923

This issue was fully paid out and examples thus rare.

Ville de Paris

Frs. 1,000 Elaborately decorated	Green/Black	1929

Recently redeemed.

City of Oaxaca (Mexico) 1910 5%

Pesos 200	Brown/Black	750
Pesos 500	Green/Black	800

AUTOMOBILES

Following the successful development of steam railways, it is not surprising that man's enthusiasm to develop a horseless vehicle was fired. But this time, it was France and not Britain, where most progress was made. The reason for this is simply a legal one, whereas Britain imposed a 10 mph speed limit and a requirement for a red flag to be carried ahead of the vehicle, France proved far more liberal.

Thus although the first petrol driven car was produced by Daimler in 1887, it was France which rapidly took the lead in building commercial quantities of vehicles. The most prominent manufacturer of the time was Messrs Panhard and Levassor, whose factory in Paris was the pride of the industry employing 850 men by 1901. Other early French companies included such famous names as 'Mors', and 'De Dion-Bouton' while 'Minerva Motors' established its reputation in building engines and conversion kits for the bicycle.

Progress was surprisingly fast in the first few years and this was greatly encouraged by the establishment of 'races'. The first of these in 1894 was sponsored by the French newspaper *Le Petit Journal* which announced 'a competition for carriages to be propelled without horses'. The course was from Paris to Rouen and entry required an ability to achieve 7¾ mph. Only three contestants lasted the course averaging 12 mph. But it was the following year which really set the standards with the inauguration of the Paris–Bordeaux–Paris race, a distance of 732 miles. Twenty-two cars took part and nine finished – a significant improvement over the previous year.

In Britain, meanwhile, attitudes were mellowing and not only was the red flag abolished but the speed limit was raised to 14 mph! To celebrate, supporters organized a procession of cars travelling from London to Brighton, and so began the famous annual event of the spring. Much of the interest in early automotive transport, not surprisingly perhaps, came from the wealthy. Such worthies as W. K. Vanderbilt, Baron Henri de Rothschild and the Hon. C. S. Rolls were active participants in races of the time. One such event, first organized in 1900, was the Gordon-Bennett Cup, named after the instigator, a wealthy newspaper proprietor. This race attracted enormous publicity and greatly encouraged competition at both the national and corporate level. A rule of entry insisted on manufacture being one hundred per cent of the country whose flag was represented.

A share certificate of a famous early car manufacturer.

The concentration of early development in France resulted in the adoption of several French words into the automobile vocabulary. 'Automobile' itself is an obvious one and others include 'garage', 'chauffeur' and 'mechanic'. But manufacture was not limited to Europe and by 1903 there were reputed to be 300 factories in the United States building mechanically driven road vehicles. In 1902 over 19,000 were produced generating a total revenue of $20 million. Such investors as Mr Baker of Cleveland, with his electrician Mr Denzer, were actively developing electrically propelled racing cars, and many other companies were preparing the way for the ultimate giants of Ford and General Motors.

Production was not limited to the private passenger vehicle, for it was seen at an early date that in order to gain widespread popularity, the general public must be involved and given the opportunity to benefit from developments. An extract from an article which appeared in the *Daily Mail* of 30 November 1897 indicates the thinking of the time: 'We hardly turn round now to look at the motor cab. This has been found perfectly practicable, perfectly comfortable, perfectly safe. It is now the turn of the motor omnibus, and from one quarter or another it is certain to arise before long. After that we pine for the motor dray. Meanwhile, it is not a bad year's record that half London has already left off laughing at a carriage without a horse; the other half will soon get tired of laughing when only one man in two sees the joke.' Most of the early omnibuses were manufactured by De Dion–Bouton et Cie and exported worldwide. Ready markets included Bolivia, USA, Italy, Austria and Spain. Several companies were established in the latter to run the vehicles, one of the most significant being the 'Sociedad Espanola de Automoviles Segovie a la Granja' which made a point of allocating one of its vehicles for the sole use of the Royal Family.

Many of the omnibus company share certificates exist today and make fascinating collecting material. Even as early as 1902 prototype armed tanks were being prepared. First attempts were little more than 'cars' surrounded by steel sheeting with guns on top but it is significant that military uses were being thought up while development work was still in its infancy. The earliest such vehicle was designed by Fred R. Simms and built by Vickers, Son & Maxim Ltd, but its first trial was not attended by the army, as *The Autocar* magazine of 1902 somewhat cynically put it: 'Doubtless they (the War Office) were most intensely employed in the alteration of a button die or in the design of some fresh form of dustman's cap, wherewith to further disfigure the Guards and alienate the nursemaid's heart. Such important matters must not be put aside for the consideration of such an airy and insignificant trifle as "Simm's motor war car".' Bureaucracy, it appears, is nothing new.

The listing of certain automobile certificates at the end of this chapter will give the collector some idea of the scope of this theme. The international appeal of 'cars' has had its effect on demand for related share certificates, however, and prices for items in this sector tend to be high. An example is the 1971 certificate of Rolls-Royce – just prior to this company's financial reorganization its shares were trading at 2½d (that's old pence!), now the certificates regularly fetch upwards of £100. There's a lesson there somewhere for all companies about to 'go down the tubes'.

SAMPLE LIST OF EXISTING AUTOMOBILE COMPANY CERTIFICATES

Rolls-Royce Ltd 1971
Durant Motors Inc. *c.* 1930
Hudson Motor Co. *c.* 1950
The Nash Motor Company *c.* 1930
Benz & Cie, Mannheim 1920
Daimler-Benz, Berlin 1934
Daimler Motoren Gesellschaft 1920
Daimler-Benz, Stuttgart 1940
Bayerische Motoren Werke, Munchen 1925
Lindcar-Auto, Berlin 1922
Skodawerke, Pilsen 1900
Steyr-Werke AG, Vienna 1926
Isotta Fraschini, Milan 1904
Hispano Suiza, Barcelona 1900
Societa Automobili Lombarda, Bergamo
Athenienne d'Automobiles 'Athena' S.A. Athens 1918
Kaiser-Frazer Corporation, Nevada 1948
S.A. Andre Citroen, Paris 1924

Usines d'Automobiles G. Brouhot, Paris 1906
Automobiles Charon Girardot & Voigt 1905
Comp. des Automobiles 'Meteor', Paris 1906
Le Sud-Automobile, Avignon 1916
Automobiles Cottin & Desgouttes, Lyon 1919
Fabrication de Automobiles Renault de Espana S.A. 'Fasa' 1968
Paris-Transport-Automobiles, Paris 1924
Soc. Nouvelle des Automobiles Martini, St Blaise 1911
Minerva Motors S.A., Berghem, Anvers 1920
Automobiles Industriels 'Sawes', Suresnes 1923
Automobiles M. Berliet. Berliet & Cie. Lyon 1943
The Poole and Sandbanks Motor Car Co. 1904
Societa Italiana Automobile DARRACQ, Naples 1906
Oesterreichischen Daimler Motoren AG. Vienna 1927
The Motor Manufacturing Co. 1898
Vulcan Motor & Engineering Co. (1906) Ltd 1920

Minerva Motors S.A. – a Belgian Motor company certificate of 1920.

SIGNATURES

For many of us, the collecting of autographs was a fundamental part of growing up. Not just anyone's autograph, of course, only those of the famous or, perhaps, the nearly famous. An autograph was not simply a material possession, it was undisputed proof of personal contact with the Great. As time passed, signatures continued to hold our fascination, but not in albums, preferably on cheques.

Capitalist motives aside, however, it continues to be the case that owning a document signed by a well-known person of the time, has an unbeatable attraction for many of the collecting fraternity. Bonds and shares lend themselves admirably to this field and the collecting of famous signatures makes an ideal theme with material crossing all frontiers.

Signatures not only enhance the certificate from an historical point of view, but can also appreciably affect its value as discussed later in the book. Recognizing a signature as famous is not always obvious and a well-informed collector can often pick up a bargain at a dealer's expense. In order to give a feel for the theme, several of the better-known signatories are dealt with in some depth in the pages which follow, whilst others are listed on page 104.

WELLS AND FARGO

Perhaps of all the famous signatories to be found on early share certificates, those of Henry Wells and William Fargo, are the most coveted. To many, they are synonymous with the opening up of America and its commercial development through the founding of the American Express Co.

Henry Wells, an ex-schoolteacher and son of a pastor, learnt the express business under William F. Harnden ('the father of express') and in 1841 formed Pomeroy & Co. which not only carried valuables and currency but, for a while, even oysters (at $3 per 100) and mail, much to the government's dismay. The business was centred on Buffalo.

In 1843 Wells met and hired W. G. Fargo as a messenger and shortly afterwards formed a partnership running an express line from Buffalo to Detroit. Eventually many of the competing companies joined forces and in March 1850, the American Express Company was formed with a capital of $150,000. It was an unincorporated association with a limited life of only ten years. A special provision prevented anyone from buying shares in the company without the board's consent, and shares could not be sold to 'married women, infants, or irresponsible persons'.

Many agreements were established with the railroad and packet boat companies. Wells was appointed President at a salary of $1,250 p.a., and in the first four months, the Company earned enough to pay a 10% dividend on capital.

The American Express Co. – a certificate hand-signed by Wells and Fargo c. 1866.

American Merchants Union Express Co., signed by William Fargo in 1869.

In 1852, Wells and Fargo wanted to expand operations to California and cash in on the gold rush, but other directors opposed the idea. As a result a new offshoot was created – 'The Wells Fargo Co.' which became the leading express company in the West. Another equally famous offshoot, 'The Overland Mail' was set up by fellow director John Butterfield running stage coaches from St Louis to San Francisco.

By 1854 the Company had increased its capital to $750,000. Business developed fast and their messengers covered 15,000 miles a day. Headquarters were established in New York and a spur track from the Hudson River Railroad Co. ran right into the ground floor permitting direct loading and unloading.

After its first ten years, and in accordance with the original terms, the Company was dissolved and the assets auctioned off. Existing shareholders successfully bid for them at a cost of $600,000.

In 1867, a major competitor was formed by a group of wealthy businessmen known as the 'Merchants Union Express Co.' The resulting price war led to both companies making substantial losses and they finally agreed to merge, forming the 'American Merchants Union Express Co.' Wells resigned as President and was succeeded by Fargo, although his younger brother, J. C. Fargo, handled most of the detail. The name was changed back to the American Express Co. in 1873 and J. C. Fargo became President in 1881.

The development of the company with its gradually increasing capitalization is clearly depicted by the share certificates and at least six different designs have been identified. Both Wells and Fargo signatures appear on the certificates, but only that of Fargo on the American Merchants Union Express Co., Wells having retired by that time.

JOHN D. ROCKEFELLER

Born in 1839, the son of a patent medicine salesman, John D. Rockefeller built up one of the largest personal fortunes in history and established the Rockefeller name on the American scene.

Like all great entrepreneurs, his success arose from a modest outlay on a new product – that product just happened to be oil. An initial $4,000 investment in a refinery in 1862 was the start of the Standard Oil Company of Ohio. In 1868, Henry Flagler joined Rockefeller and by 1870 the Company was incorporated at $1 million. The 10,000 shares were owned by Rockefeller, Andrews, Flagler and Harkness.

Refining 1,500 barrels a day, the Company became the world's largest oil producer. It rapidly acquired most of the country's refineries and by 1880, controlled 90% of the US oil business. Following a series of anti-trust cases the Company was eventually broken up in 1911.

Between 1875 and 1882 when the Company increased its capital from $1 million to $3.5 million, the share certificates bear the signatures of Rockefeller and Flagler. As the number of shareholders was tightly controlled (only five in 1870 and forty-one in 1880) very few such certificates are believed to exist and as a consequence, tend to fetch consistently high prices at auction.

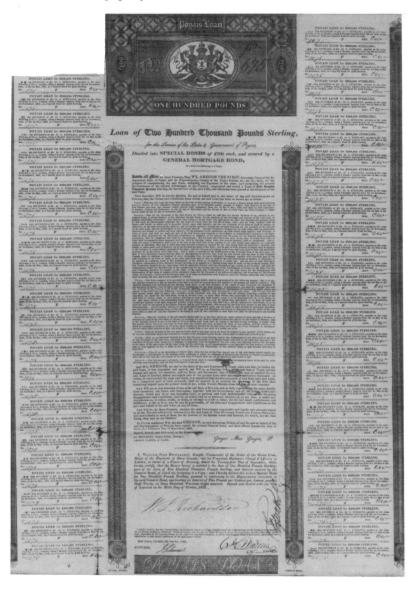

Above: *A £100 bond in the 'State of Poyais'.*

Right: *An early share certificate in the Standard Oil Company (SO, later Esso) signed by the original Rockefeller in 1878.*

Opposite above: *Mission Development Co. – facsimile signature of Paul Getty.*

Opposite below: *The Getty Oil Company was a follow-up to Mission Development – it also shows a facsimile signature of the founder Paul Getty.*

GREGOR MACGREGOR, CACIQUE OF POYAIS

Appealing signatures do not always have to be those of upright men or women. The infamous can be as attractive as the famous; such is that of Gregor Macgregor.

A Scottish mercenary of the early nineteenth century, Macgregor rose to the rank of General in the Venezuelan army. He was instrumental in the expulsion of the Spanish and together with a small force landed in a swampy mosquito-infested area of Nicaragua. There he 'negotiated' land rights with the primitive inhabitants and in 1821 sailed for England where he was able to transfix his audiences with fabulous tales of the wonderful kingdom of 'Poyais'.

The discontented populace of the time were enthused by his revelations and were soon pressing to emigrate. Macgregor, self-styled 'Cacique of Poyais' began selling land grants and local currency notes, raising £200,000 in 1822 with the aid of respected London bankers, Perring & Co. This was followed by a further issue of £300,000 in Paris in 1825.

Many set sail to find their Utopia but on arrival were met with tropical heat, disease, hurricanes and little else. Despite brave attempts by the Governor of British Honduras to rescue the duped settlers, over 200 died.

In 1827 Macgregor was imprisoned in England but shortly released, implying the involvement of more well known establishment figures. A similar spell in a French prison was followed by his retirement to Venezuela where he was reinstated to his former army rank and, on death, granted full military honours.

The shareholder certificates and land grants often bear the signature of Gregor Macgregor which greatly adds to their glamour. But, signatures aside, the documents make fascinating and amusing reading and make us appreciate the ease of perpetrating fraud in a world only just entering the era of fast communications.

THE COMMODORE – CORNELIUS VANDERBILT

It would be remiss in a section devoted to famous signatures to omit reference to at least one of the great 'Railway Barons', and, while the name of Vanderbilt may only conjure up a pair of jeans to the modern generation, to most of us the name is synonymous with the development of the US Railroads.

Starting with $100 Vanderbilt began his career in shipping. While in his twenties he ordered the first steamship and eventually controlled a sizeable fleet. Seeing the beginnings and advantages of railroads, he purchased the Harlem Railroad and extended it to Manhattan. After this came the Hudson River RR Co. and, eventually, the New York Central. His business deals bore the true marks of an entrepreneur of the time – deviousness and unscrupulousness – but nevertheless effective.

His son, William Henry, and grandsons, Cornelius and William Kissam, all followed the Commodore into the railroad empire. Their signatures appear on many certificates including the New York and Harlem, the Canada Southern and the New York Central.

Space does not permit full credit to all the famous signatures gracing bonds and shares. Many of these are therefore only listed, but even this does not purport to be comprehensive and is only indicative of the scope of this most fascinating collecting theme.

SIGNATURE	CERTIFICATE
Henry Wells & William Fargo	American Express Co. (1850–70)
John D. Rockefeller	Standard Oil Co. (1870s)
J. Paul Getty (facsimile)	Mission Development Co. (1950s)
Bernie Cornfield (facsimile)	I.O.S. (1960s)
Gregor Macgregor	Poyais (c. 1820–30)
Commodore Cornelius Vanderbilt	New York & Harlem RR
Robert Morris	North American Land Co. (c. 1795)
Whittaker Wright	London & Globe Co.
Stephen Austin	Texian Loan, 1836
Thomas Edison	Edison Portland Cement Co. (c. 1899)
Abe Bailey	Du Preez Gold Mining
Johann Strauss	Der Comische Oper
George Pullman	Pullman's Palace Car Co. (c. 1869)

MINING

Second only to railways in terms of volume and variety of material, mining offers the collector a vast area from which may be selected specific themes, such as minerals, areas or periods.

It would be wrong to think of gold and diamonds as the only alternative. Copper, tin, silver, coal and lead are all equally interesting and in this chapter we hope to touch on them all, some in more depth than others.

GOLD

Throughout the centuries, gold has always held a unique fascination. It has been the most sought after element, at times involving thousands of hopeful prospectors. Inevitably this constant searching resulted in the formation of many companies and the subsequent issue of a large variety of related share certificates. Although the mining of gold goes back many centuries, the issue of share certificates does not, and for that reason we must concentrate on the period from the mid-nineteenth century, when gold was first discovered and mined on a significant commercial scale.

The great 'Gold Rush' began in 1848 in California. Gold was discovered by James W. Marshall close by his partner's ranch at Sutters Fort. At the time, San Francisco boasted a population of 800 and it was only one year after the state of California had been transferred to America from Mexico.

News of the discovery spread fast and prospectors travelled from all over the world to try their hand – they became known as the 'forty-niners' and swelled the population of California from 26,000 to 115,000 in the space of a year. Difficulties of travel and doubts over successful discoveries on arrival led to the grouping together of the prospectors, often under the umbrella of a company. For this reason many of the companies of the period formed to mine gold in California, were in fact registered elsewhere. Examples are:

The Ave Maria Gold Quartz Mine, registered in London in 1851.
The Anglo Californian Gold Mining Co., registered in London in 1852.
Le Nouveau Monde, registered in both London and Paris in 1851.
Advantages of forming a company were not only limited to a sharing of risks and rewards, but it also gave the opportunity for investors, not personally wishing to travel, to invest from a distance.

The frantic scramble for gold in the 1850s inevitably led to social problems, not the least of which was racial strife – a feature to be repeated in most of the major gold mining areas. However, apart from the unfortunate aspects, a great many positive features developed. One of these was much improved mining techniques, particularly in the area of alluvial mining. Although not a mining company, the share certificate of the Toulomne County Water Co. (1854) beautifully portrays the alluvial process. One of the immigrant miners was Edward Hargraves from England, although originally from Australia. He recalled mountains of a similar shape to those being mined in California from his Australian childhood and so set off to seek

Alluvial miners are shown at work in the vignette on this Unity Mining Company unissued certificate.

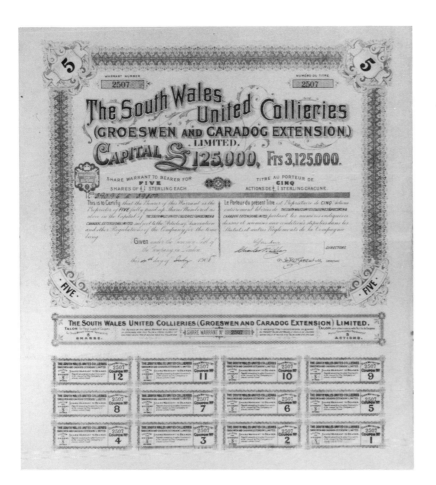

Opposite above: *The Lead and Zinc Mine of Tunisia – bearer share of 1924.*

Opposite below: *A certificate for 25 shares in the Cariboo Quartz Mining Co.*

Left: *The South Wales United Collieries Ltd – bearer share of 1908.*

Below: *A share certificate of the Liverton Ironstone Co. Ltd dated 1869.*

them out. He discovered gold in New South Wales, Australia in 1851. The development process was much the same as California with frantic searching and large influxes of foreigners, but many of the techniques learnt in the United States were successfully adopted in Australia. Typical companies of the time were the British Australia Gold Mining Co. (1851) and the Lake Bathurst Australasian Gold Mining Co.

The third major area of discovery was South Africa. Gold was discovered at Witwatersrand, in the Transvaal, in 1886, but unlike California and Australia, it was difficult and costly to mine thus necessitating the establishment of a more organized commercial approach at an early stage. Many companies were formed and several of these have been referred to in the chapter on South Africa. The companies were mostly registered in London or on the gold fields themselves at the local stock exchanges of Kimberley and Barberton – for example, the Consort Reef Gold Mining Co. Ltd of 1890.

Gold discoveries were not limited to the three areas briefly described here and the scripophilist who chooses this theme will find fascinating material from Mexico to the Far East. Space unfortunately limits us from expounding further on this most glamorous of metals.

DIAMONDS

Much has already been said about the diamond mines of South Africa in an earlier chapter. This area is obviously the most important outside the Soviet Union and consequently there are relatively few certificates from other countries concerned with this theme. An interesting exception is the Société Miniere Intercoloniale of the Central African Republic. Remember those diamonds reputed to have been 'given' to a French President by Emperor Bokassa? Well, that's where they came from.

COPPER

Copper deposits were far more common than gold or diamonds and the choice of certificates is consequently much more varied. The largest producing region in Europe in the latter part of the nineteenth century was Devon and Cornwall in Great Britain. The Devon Great Consols Mine produced over £3 million worth of ore between 1844 and 1864. Copper was also actively mined in South Africa, Australia, the United States and Scandinavia. An attractive certificate of the latter is that of Langterns Koppargrufvor of 1907.

TIN

Without doubt the centre of tin mining in the early 1800s was Cornwall. Presence of the deposits led to the region becoming a major area of industrialization and the workings resulted in the development of much advanced equipment. One of the most significant such offshoot was steam traction and it was the son of the manager of the Dolcoath Mine, Richard Trevithick, who built the first steam locomotive.

Other tin mining areas included Nigeria, the Far East and Australia.

OTHER MINERALS

Whether your interests are with lead, silver or coal, there is no doubt that there is adequate interesting material on which to develop a collection. Mining often formed the nucleus of social and economic progress in a community and for this reason it is a particularly interesting field in which to specialize. The material is often extremely attractive and was usually held by relatively small groups of people, thus limiting the quantities issued of individual types.

The mining company shares illustrated here will give a good idea of the scope available.

*A Swedish copper mine
certificate of 1907.*

BANKS

First thoughts might indicate that the theme of banking may, in scope, lag considerably behind that of mining. One statistic alters that view; since 1700, over 3,120 banks have been registered in the United Kingdom *alone*. Most, of course, crashed, amalgamated or disappeared, but nevertheless all would have raised capital through the issue of share certificates, debentures or other financial instruments. With the addition of other countries, particularly the United States, France, Germany, Russia and South Africa, the total number of banks facing the potential collector is likely to exceed 10,000.

At this point you may be feeling that the theme is too large, and indeed it does appear frightening at first glance, but there are several factors which considerably reduce the amount of scrip available for collection. The most significant of these is that banks, being banks, were rather more careful about leaving behind quantities of share certificates whether issued or unissued, bearer or registered. Most were therefore destroyed, as should have been the case with other companies, but financial good housekeeping was not always the speciality of more adventurous institutions and their entrepreneurial founders. Strange as it may be, there are in fact, relatively few bank share certificates around, and the author believes that assembling a collection of 500 different types would present even the most determined collector with a difficult task.

In this chapter we are primarily concerned with bank scrip *per se*, namely certificates issued by the bank to finance itself; we are not so concerned with the share and bond issues raised by a particular bank (or banks) on behalf of another company or government. However, as the two areas are obviously related, a word or two on the subject may be appropriate.

BANKS AS AGENTS, UNDERWRITERS AND MANAGERS

An earlier chapter in Part 1 touched on the involvement of banks in international bond issues. A country or company seeking to borrow large amounts of money from worldwide lenders may well not have the international recognition of a bank. The bank thus acts as a figurehead of respectability for the borrower and appends its name (as Agent, Manager or Underwriter) to each bond.

Examples of such endorsements are the following:

COUNTRY	LOAN	BANKS
China	1908 5% Gold Loan	Hongkong & Shanghai Banking Corporation and Banque de l'Indo Chine
	1919 8% Vickers Loan	Lloyds Bank Limited
Germany	Free State of Saxony 1927	Hambros Bank Limited
Russia	City of Nicolaiev 1912 5%	National Westminster Bank and Royal Bank of Scotland

Some may argue that the inclusion of a bank's name on a bond subsequently defaulted places some responsibility for compensation on the bank to those who purchased the bond on the reputation of the Agent. The banks would argue otherwise.

Today, as in the past, there is considerable competition amongst banks to be seen to be acting as Agent and for leading a major international loan. An interesting tale of such competition surrounds the Chinese Reorganization Loan of 1913.

As mentioned earlier the loan was required to bolster the government against civil disturbance. It was seen by the great powers as of major political importance. Discussions with the Chinese on the terms of the loan were long and difficult being handled by banking syndicates from Britain, France, Germany and the USA. The Chartered Bank made concerted efforts to get in on the act but were rebutted by the leading British bank (Hongkong & Shanghai) and the Foreign Office. Early in 1912, Japan and Russia joined the consortium but the negotiations continued to be difficult and encouraged the Chinese to sound the market elsewhere. As a result another loan was signed in 1912 – The Crisp Loan – so named after a firm of stockbrokers responsible for its construction. The Chartered Bank was involved in this loan but the British Foreign Office was so incensed by its success that pressure was put on the Chinese to cancel half of the authorized amount of £10 million. The Crisp Loan was secured against salt revenues and imposed far less

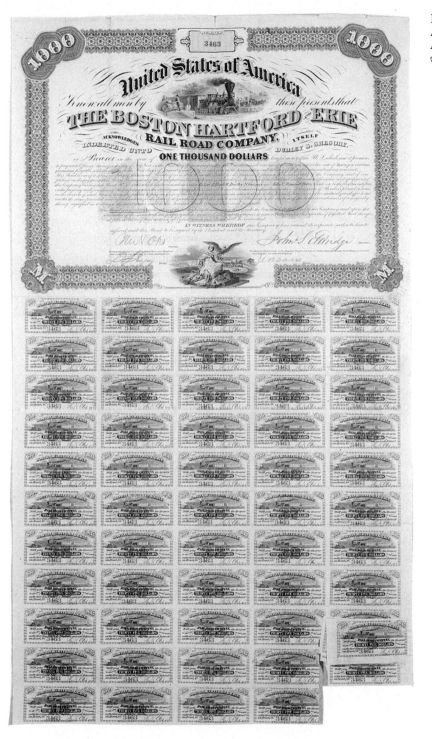

Left: *A $1,000 bond of the Boston Hartford and Erie Rail Road issued in 1866 bearing a vignette of an early loco.*

*The Barcelona Traction Light &
Power Co. – a Canadian
registered company nationalized
without compensation.*

controls on the Chinese than the much discussed Reorganization Loan. The latter was eventually signed but caused considerable unpopularity in China as it was seen as further evidence of continued and increasing foreign control.

The inclusion of bonds on the basis of an issuing bank, certainly widens the scope of the Banking theme, but the true collector of banking scrip will almost certainly prefer the certificates issued in the name of the banks themselves. We therefore return to this area and without attempting to be comprehensive, select a few examples which may whet the interest of prospective collectors.

RUSSIA

A great many banks operated in Russia prior to the Revolution. The two most well known were the Peasants Land Bank and the Land Bank of the Nobility. Each was concerned with the problems of transferring land from nobility to serfs, although from different sides of the fence, and both were major issuers of bonds subsequently defaulted in 1917. As may be considered appropriate, the Nobility's default exceeded the Peasants' by the ratio of about 9:1, but together they accounted for nearly £100 million of Russia's bad debts. There is no shortage of material relating to these banks although the higher denomination bonds are often harder to obtain for the collector.

A particularly interesting story concerning the Bank of Siberia and others, has recently come to light, which highlights the close relationship of scripophily and history – in this case, history of political intrigue. The story surfaced shortly after the author had been mysteriously offered 2,400 share certificates of the Commercial Bank of Siberia, by no less a body than Her Majesty's Treasury.

It appears that during the latter days of World War I, considerable concern was being expressed by Britain that the Russian war effort against Germany was in danger of collapse as the Revolution began to take hold. British officers were sent to Russia with three objectives: one – to keep allied armaments out of German hands; two – to ensure continued supplies of funds to the one remaining loyal fighting unit – the Cossacks; and three – to do everything possible to ensure Britain's continued benefits from close commercial liaison with Russia after the war.

The British envoy presented with this task was General Poole and he conceived a plan of taking over the Russian economy through the purchase of five of the major Commercial banks; the Russian Bank for Foreign Trade, the International Bank, the Commercial and Industrial Bank, the Volga-Kana Bank, and the Siberian Bank.

The takeover plan was approved by the British Government and funds were approved, but the implementation was confounded by the Bolsheviks smelling a rat, the Germans trying to do the same thing, and the tendency for large sums of money to 'go missing'. At the end of the day majority shareholdings were achieved in two of the target banks and a deposit of £300,000 paid on the Siberian bank with an agreement to pick up the balance after the war. The overall objective was to control the Russian grain trade and thus, the economy.

Inevitably the Revolution put a stop to these intrigues and the banks' assets were confiscated by the State. The tale does not end there, however, for the owner of the Siberian Bank turned up in London after the war and demanded the agreed balance of £3 million for his shares. The Treasury paid up. The author's offer to buy the shares sixty-three years later for a derisory amount was refused on the grounds that they were valued higher by the Treasury – presumably £3 million.

CHINA

Some mention has already been made of China in a banking connection but in view of the extremely attractive nature of their certificates it may be worth adding a little more comment.

Nearly all banks in China were foreign controlled and often established as a consortium to develop foreign trade. Some of this consortia could not be truly described as banks proper, but nevertheless they often raised capital for specific projects and acted as Agents for bond issues.
Examples are:

LOAN	BANK/SYNDICATE
1905 Honan Railway	The Peking Syndicate
1913 Lung-Tsing-U-Hai Railway	Compagnie Generale de Chemins de Fer et de Tramways en Chine

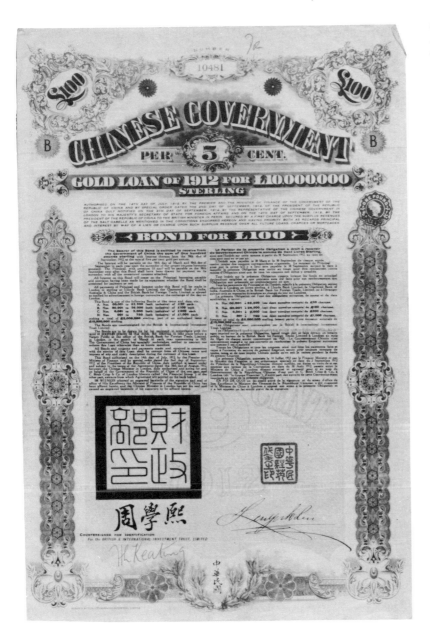

Opposite: *The Commercial Bank of Siberia – a bearer share of 1912.*

Left: *A Chinese bond for £100 – part of the 1912 'Crisp' Loan.*

The other banks were less project-related, namely, the Banque Industrielle de Chine and the Banque de Cochinchine. The surviving certificates of each are classics of their era.

UNITED STATES

US banking laws still prohibit across-state banking, thus resulting in the presence of a large number of different institutions. Early days of poor communications compounded this number by the establishment of many small (one branch) community banks, hundreds of which still exist operating rather more like an English corner shop than a bank.

The collector is thus presented with a wide choice. Names such as the Bank of Charleston, the Barnstable Bank or the Morris Canal and Banking Co. are just three of many. Like all American material, the certificates are attractively printed and often carry the signatures of famous financiers.

A large number of state banks sprang up in the early part of the nineteenth century and by 1815 as many as 208 were in operation. Their strength largely followed from the failure of the first 'Bank of the United States' and it was not until 1816 that the 'Second Bank of the United States' was created to act as a Central bank, twenty per cent owned by the Government. Nicholas Biddle was made the third president but later conflicts with Andrew Jackson resulted in its eventual collapse.

OTHER COUNTRIES

Lack of space prevents further country by country detail but references have frequently been made to banking issues in the country theme chapters. The listing which follows emphasizes the theme's scope which extends from Egypt to South America.

A SAMPLE LISTING OF BANK CERTIFICATES

CHINA

Banque Industrielle de Chine
3 issues c. 1919. Black/Yellow
1 issue Blue/Black. Very ornate.

Banque de Cochinchine
Founder's share Brown/Red
Registered share c. 1908. Red (rare)
Both types depict Chinese scenes.

GREAT BRITAIN

The Cheque Bank Limited
Guarantee obligation £100. c. 1876. Green/ White.

The Anglo-South American Bank Ltd
c. 1930. Now Lloyds International Bank.

The Million Bank
Stock receipt c. 1752

The New Oriental Bank Corporation Ltd
£10 share c. 1885. Coat of arms. Black/Green.

PALESTINE

The Mizrahi Bank Ltd, Jerusalem.
Bearer share certificate issued in 1924. Attractive with Blue/Brown ornate border. Printed in English and Hebrew.

Agrobank Ltd
Agricultural and building bank for Palestine. 1930 debenture in Green/Beige. Unusual border and bank crest at corners.

The Workers Bank Ltd
Incorporated under the laws of Erez-Israel. 1935 share certificate. Blue/Cream with Red seal showing Star of David.

EUROPE

Banco Industrial y Mercantil (Spain)
Share certificate for 2,000 Reales c. 1864.

Banque d'Orient (Greece)
1904 share certificate for 125 gold francs.

Banque Nationale de Grece
Certificate of 1904. 200 Drachmas

German Central Bank of Agriculture
6% bond $1,000 c. 1927. Yellow/Black.

American-Serbian Credit Bank for Colonization, Trade and Industry
c. 1923 share. Brown/Blue.

Neuer Wiener Bankgesellshaft
c. 1923 bearer share, Brown/Cream

Stockholms Enskilda Bank
Various denominations. c. 1950

AUSTRALIA

Bank of Australia
£100 share c. 1833

Mercantile Bank of Australia Ltd
Share in Black/White. c. 1891

OTHER COUNTRIES

Banco Central Mexicano
Extremely attractive share certificate in Green/ Black with printed Red revenue stamp. Mexican eagle and lakeside views. Coupons attached. 1908.

Banco Territoria y Agricola de Puerto-Rico
7% Bond. 100 Pesos. c. 1895

Credit Foncier Agricole du Maroc
Bearer share. Elaborate Moorish design. 1920

For Russian material see page 61 and United States of America, pages 79–81.

SHIPPING

Travel on water is perhaps the oldest mode of transport devised by man. This chapter limits such transport to overseas shipping thus excluding the equally fascinating subject of inland waterways which is briefly touched upon later.

No doubt interest in shipping arises both from thoughts of exotic destinations and sails billowing in the wind. Our interest is a little more mercenary for we are concerned with the companies themselves which were responsible for the building and managing of the great shipping fleets of the world. The theme, so far as the scripophilist is concerned, is narrowed further by beginning with the introduction of steam and the demise of sail. The author apologizes to all those seeking tales of Viking long boats and their spoils.

THE BIRTH OF STEAM

Although early experiments were carried out in France at the end of the seventeenth century, it was in Britain, or, to be more exact, Scotland, where the most significant developments took place. In 1787 W. Miller published a thesis on alternatives to wind and although his initial solution was paddle wheels driven by manpower, his associate, James Taylor, developed the idea and substituted a steam engine. The first successful test took place in 1788 on Dalswinton Loch, Scotland, where a speed of 5 mph was achieved.

In the United States, Robert Fulton, having witnessed the Scottish experiments, built the *Clermont*, a successful steamer which regularly plied the Hudson River between Albany and New York, a distance of 142 miles, in 32 hours. Henry Bell built a similar ship in 1812, the *Comet*, which sailed the Clyde from Glasgow. After this date, many ships were built on the Clyde and cross-channel services to Ireland began in 1816. A major improvement was the substitution of a screw propeller for the paddle wheel and this development was crucial in persuading the Admiralty to adopt steam driven ships for the Navy.

As steam ships became a more accepted animal and their benefits of speed and size realized, their adoption into the trading companies was inevitable. The close relationship between ship builders and line managers stemmed from those early days in Scotland and the story of the Elder Dempster Company is a perfect example of development in the nineteenth century. The tale is made more interesting for the scripophilist by the ready availability of share certificates in the company and its associates.

ELDER DEMPSTER COMPANY

Although trade with West Africa initially concentrated on the profitable business of slave trading, it was the availability of other produce, particularly vegetable oils, which was primarily responsible for its growth in importance to the European markets.

The African Steam Ship Company founded by Royal Charter in 1852 was the first shipping company to establish regular links with the region. Its prime objective was to carry mail for the British Government, for which it was amply rewarded. 11,008 partly-paid shares of £20 each were issued and the managing director was Macgregor Laird.

Laird's father founded the shipbuilding company later to become 'Cammell Laird & Co.', while his mother was the daughter of our old friend Gregor Macgregor of Poyais! In its first year the company made a profit of £3,486 but following Laird's death the board erred on the side of caution and this led to the formation of a more aggressive competitor – the British and African Steam Navigation Co. The company was formed in 1868 with a nominal capital of £200,000.

Two ex-employees of the African Steamship Co. were appointed agents for the new line; their names were John Dempster and Alexander Elder. The Elder Dempster Co. was thus formed in 1868. Sixteen years later the founders retired and their senior clerk, Alfred Jones, took control. Jones was eventually able to act as agent for both shipping groups and thus pulled together the whole West African trade.

On Jones's death, Lords Kylsant and Pirie (the former a director of the Royal Mail Steam Packet Co. and the latter chairman of Harland and Wolff) bought Elder Dempster from the executor for £500,000 through the establishment of Elder Dempster and Company Limited in 1910. This company, of which many share certificates exist today, was financed by the issue of 500,000 £1 cumulative preference shares, 400,000 £1 ordinary shares, 10,000 £1 management shares and £1 million of 5% debentures.

Right: *The African Steam Ship Co. – formed in 1852 and the forerunner to colonial trade with West Africa.*

Below: *Compagnie Maritime de la Seine – founder's share of 1899 with views of London and Paris.*

Opposite: *Elder Dempster & Co. Ltd – a preference share certificate of 1922.*

Having pulled together the lines of Elder Dempster and the Royal Mail Steam Packet Co., Lord Kylsant set out on a process of acquisition, which eventually included sizeable stakes in Lamport and Holt, the Union Castle Steamship Co. and the White Star Line (owner of the Titanic).

But all did not go well for Kylsant and following depressed trade, a management fallout and City rumours of insolvency, the group collapsed in 1931. The first to go was Lamport & Holt and Kylsant was convicted of giving false information in a prospectus.

Following a complex restructuring process the company was reconstituted in 1936 under the name 'Elder Dempster Lines Holdings Ltd' and is now part of Ocean Transport and Trading Ltd.

CERTIFICATES FOR COLLECTORS

Concentrating on one particular group of companies in the wide world of shipping, may perhaps have given an impression of narrow scope for the collector. This is certainly not the case as similar stories of development, takeover and liquidation exist for most of the major shipping lines. Choosing a particular line, such as Elder Dempster can be a collecting theme in itself and there are no doubt at least fifty different certificates relating to this company's history alone.

Other countries where shipping has played an important part are the United States, Scandinavia and Greece. In the case of the former the shipping companies involved in the Confederate 'Blockade' make a fascinating historical theme.

OTHER THEMES

To say that there are as many themes as fish in the sea would be something of an exaggeration, but nevertheless there are a considerable number and to present a chapter on each would keep the reader in literary chains for many moons. For this reason I have decided to provide a brief paragraph of certain of the major uncovered themes and simply list a further assortment.

OIL

Reference has already been made to the Standard Oil Co. on page 101, and the subject is clearly a very topical one, but mineral oil (as opposed to vegetable oil) is not only a recent phenomenon. Discoveries, and subsequently, oil companies, go back to the mid-nineteenth century and although most were small companies from the United States, several other countries such as Russia, Nigeria and Mexico are also able to boast of relatively early involvement as demonstrated by a number of share certificates.

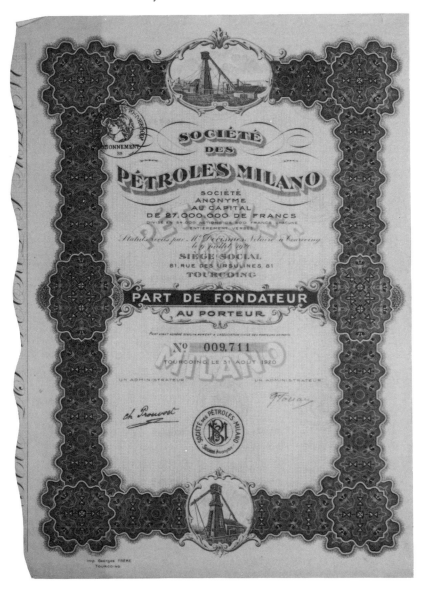

The Italian Oil Company registered in France.

ENTERTAINMENT

The world of entertainment is a wide one and any collector choosing this field must be clear on his horizons. Stretching from hotels through casinos, theatres, cinemas and clubs, the subject can be both amusing and exasperating in its sheer size.

CANALS

Throughout the various thematic chapters, canals has been a subject regularly raised, but often, as very much a second string to railways. Canal certificates are both numerous and intriguing. Many are dated around the late eighteenth century and often bear interesting seals or vignettes. France, Britain and the United States were big builders of canals but do not forget the classics of Panama, Corinth and Suez.

HERALDRY

A great many bonds and shares carry heraldic devices, usually with the intention of adding authenticity to their monetary objectives. Some such as the Russian City bonds are correctly displayed, whereas others, such as those of Poyais, are a mere fabrication designed to impress. There are many stringent rules governing the portrayal of coats of arms and an incorrect display is often indicative of a shady concern. The collector of this theme must combine the knowledge of two hobbies in order to maximize his benefit, but the end result can be most interesting.

OTHERS

It is not intended that the following list should be taken as comprehensive and indeed permutations could considerably add to the overall length of options; nevertheless, the broad scope of scripophily is indicated:

Agriculture	Horses	Music & Art	Textiles
Aeroplanes	Insurance	Photography	Theatres
Buildings	Land	Publishing	Tobacco
Coal	Lighting	Radio	Toys
Events	Lumber	Retail Sales	Trade Associations
Exhibitions	Medical	Rubber	Tramways
Fish & Fishing	Metals & Iron	Sports	Water
Food	Movies	Sugar	Wine
Glass	Munitions	Telephones	

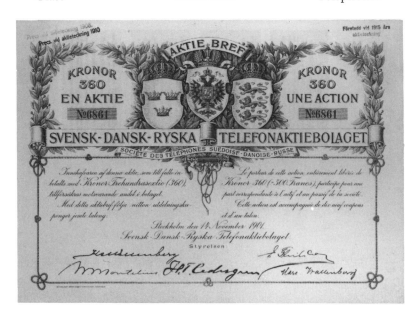

The Swedish-Danish-Russian Telephone Co. a fine example of heraldry in scripophily, it depicts the coat of arms of all three countries.

Right: *A Canadian oil field depicted on this 1934 certificate of Paramount Oils Ltd.*

Below: *Whitehead Aircraft Ltd – a famous early aircraft company. Signed by the Whitehead brothers, 1918.*

Left: *A large £20 bond in the Rio de Janeiro Suburban Tramways. 16,250 were issued in 1911 and the Company went bust in 1934.*

Below: *The Pennsylvania Canal Co. – $1,000 bond of 1870.*

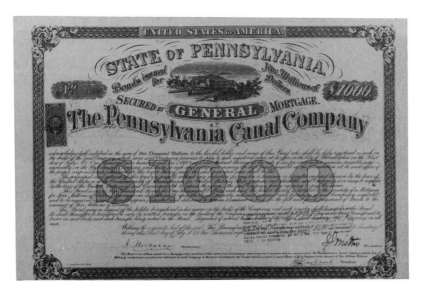

PART 3

Developing a collection

WHAT TO LOOK FOR AND WHAT TO AVOID

Part 2 provided a wide selection of themes on which to base a collection. The number presented was certainly not comprehensive and you may, for example, decide to collect by period (pre-1850 perhaps) or simply go for the best across the board. Whatever your decision, the first stage in starting a collection is to select that theme, this will allow you greater concentration and ultimately a greater expertise in your subject.

In this chapter we look at the major features of bonds and shares which assist in determining relative value. There are five determinants of value:

    Condition
    Rarity
    Age
    Signature
    Attractiveness

High value does not necessarily imply high price; like beauty, it is in the eye of the beholder. The emphasis is on *relative* value. Nevertheless, it goes without saying that a rare certificate, pre-1850, in excellent condition with a fine vignette and signed by Napoleon, would fetch a high price.

In view of the importance of the five determinants, each will be covered at some length. Their order implies no ranking in importance.

1 CONDITION

In the early days of scripophily, condition was not considered an important factor. Emphasis was placed on rarity, and poor condition was often treated as the norm for particular issues. To some extent this was understandable, bonds as bearer items have undergone considerable handling during their active life. At each transaction they were sorted and passed between offices; their large size will have necessitated folding and changing interest rates may have involved the attachment of new coupon sheets in place of the old. Smaller issues, such as the Chinese Marconi, changed hands more frequently, there being less pieces of paper to deal with, and similarly the higher denomination bonds experienced greater usage, it being far easier for a broker to count two £1,000 bonds than twenty £100 bonds. So it is important when looking at condition to bear these points in mind and it is almost essential to determine condition relative to the issue itself. Below-average condition should never be the sole reason for declining an item; it is quite possible that certain issues will always be found to be of poor quality. The reason for poor condition may be summarized as follows:

Poor quality paper.
Small size of the total loan.
High denomination, e.g. £500 or £1,000.
Age.
Physical size of the certificate itself.

The decision of whether or not to purchase an item of dubious condition must take full account of these factors in the context of the overall collection and although it is always preferable to obtain perfection, facts must be faced if such is non-existent for one or more of the above reasons. It is often better to purchase what is available (at favourable prices) and at a later date trade in the item for a better piece on that coming to light.

Although not intended to be comprehensive, the following list itemizes certain bonds and shares which are often of below-average condition.

ISSUE	REASON FOR CONDITION
Chinese 1898 4% Gold Loan	Large format. Over 80 years old.
Chinese 1918 Marconi	Poor paper. Small issue.
City of Moscow 1908, £500	High denomination. Well traded.
City of Riga 1913	Almost wholly repaid; those still around have had considerable battering from man and mouse.
Russian 1822 Rothschild	Soft paper. Very early.
Confederate Bonds	Over 120 years old, usually on poor paper. Condition varies.
Pre-1860 US Rail shares	Age and heavy cancellation marks.

At the other extreme is unissued material. Many collectors shy away from unissued shares and bonds; the lack of signatures, embossed company seals, revenue stamps and dirty thumb prints somehow give a feeling of unreality, but in point of fact, it is usually unissued material which is rarer than the issued. Unissued certificates were held as reserve stock to cover the registration of new shareholders or the

The Middleton & Tonge Cotton Mill Co. Ltd – share certificate of 1872.

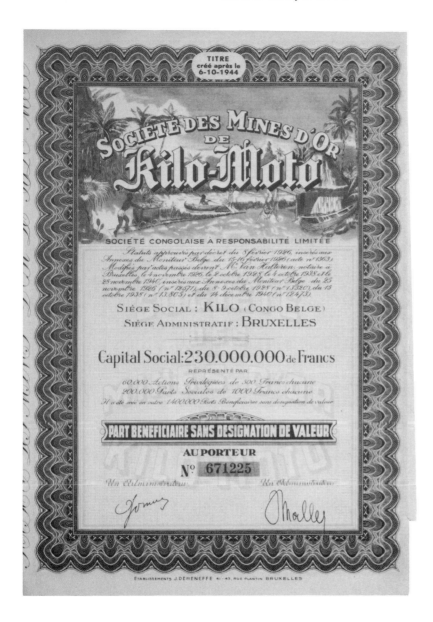

Opposite: *Almost all Japanese Government bonds have been or are being repaid. Those remaining are all the scarcer and often very attractive as illustrated here. The design shows no Japanese influence, it was printed by Waterlow & Sons of London.*

Left: *The Colonial Gold Mining Co. in the Belgian Congo (Kilo-Moto).*

replacement of lost certificates. To be technically correct, those certificates with a serial number are simply 'unissued', and those without are 'reserve stock' – the latter kept for issue as 'duplicates' and therefore given the same number as the original.

As scripophily has developed, so have levels of sophistication and attention has naturally focused on the establishment of a descriptive scale of condition. Bearing in mind earlier comments, and as a general guide only, the following gives the grades of condition and indicates the kind of price differences which may be expected according to scale:

DESCRIPTION	CONDITION	PRICE INDEX
Extremely Fine (EF)	some minor folds, clean, almost unused	100
Very Fine (VF)	some folds and creases, slight wear	85–90
Fine (F)	circulated and worn, but very slight damage	50–55
Poor (P)	much used, with some damage	10–20

The scale above tends to be used by most dealers and auction houses, but, *caveat emptor* – always inspect before purchase.

2 RARITY

What makes a certificate rare? The answer lies in one or more of the following:

FEATURE	EXAMPLE
High demand	Rockefeller signed shares of Standard Oil
Low initial issue	Coquimbo Railway (Chile)
High level of redemption	1908 5% Chinese Government loan
Old age	Canterbury & Sandwich Harbour Co. 1826

A certificate which falls into only one of the above categories although rare, is unlikely to carry a high value. Most quality pieces have at least two of the above attributes. The Standard Oil certificate, for example, not only bears a famous signature, but is also dated 1875 and believed to be limited to around 600 pieces. At the other extreme is the Russian 1894 3½% Gold Loan, 2nd issue, Frs. 12,500, of which only six bonds were issued – interest in Russian State bonds is still in its infancy and consequently such an item will not, at this stage, command a high price.

Because of this, it is unwise to buy solely for reasons of rarity. High demand is essential if the main objective is capital appreciation, and remember also, the rarer a piece the smaller will be the market in that item and unless seen from time to time at auction, its very existence will be forgotten.

This latter point is also important in determining your collecting theme. Unless highly determined (and wealthy) it can be discouraging to choose a sector of such scarcity that its constituents rarely appear. But, having said this, nearly all sectors contain certain items which are rare, and chasing these – at the right price – can prove to be the most satisfying part of building a collection.

In order to demonstrate the difficulty of achieving a complete collection, three themes have been selected and the maximum number of complete collections possible has been estimated:

COLLECTION THEME	MAXIMUM No. OF COLLECTIONS
Chinese Bonds 1898–1937 (excludes unissued & fully redeemed items)	17
Russian Cities	11
Confederate Bonds	50

It is, unfortunately, impossible to extend the exercise to cover shares, as apart from bearer items the number issued is unknown. The above are startlingly low figures in the context of the world collector population.

It is difficult to quantify rarity in a generalized table as, like condition, it has to be judged within the context of the sector. For guidance only, the following may be helpful:

SECTOR	RARITY CLASSIFICATION BY No. OF CERTIFICATES EXISTING/ISSUED		
	Extremely Rare	*Very Rare*	*Rare*
Chinese Bonds	Less than 20	21–200	201–500
Russian Cities	Less than 20	21–275	276–500
Russian Railways	Less than 100	101–300	301–500
US Railroads	Less than 100	101–300	301–500
Confederate Bonds	Less than 300	301–500	501–750
Early shares (pre-1850)	Less than 250	251–500	501–750

Rarity must always be balanced with condition and demand, and never taken in isolation as a determinant of value.

3 AGE

In the case of registered share certificates, age is, without doubt, the major determinant of value, adding both historical interest and the likelihood of fewer certificates having survived the ravages of time.

Anything dated pre-1850 may be considered very early, and pre-1800, extremely early and rare. The number of companies existing before 1800 was negligible and consequently any related material is most unusual. There are, of course, certain sectors where age is largely irrelevant. Chinese bonds, for example, all date between 1896 and 1937 and Russian Cities between 1875 and 1915. Against the advantage of history, however, one must always offset condition, and a badly torn certificate of almost any age is seldom of much value, and although professional repairs can produce a transformation it should always be clearly stated if a bond or certificate has been treated for damage.

4 SIGNATURES

This feature has been largely covered in the earlier section on collecting themes, but it is worth emphasizing the value of famous signatures. It is easy, particularly in the early years of the hobby, to overlook a signature. Remember, share certificates are often signed on both front and back, and it is always worth checking names carefully. A well-known figure in South African history may be unknown to a collector of US Railroads and vice-versa. A famous signature can increase the value by up to ten times, which makes careful scrutiny well worth while.

5 ATTRACTIVENESS

A great many bonds and shares were issued in Central Europe during the nineteenth century, often in low quantities, but because of their unattractiveness they have no demand.

Certainly not a sole factor in the setting of value, attractiveness nevertheless contributes greatly to the overall interest and appeal of a certificate. But, a word of warning, do not pay high prices purely on the strength of beauty. If the item is new to you, check the numbers issued; if not stated on the certificate itself, a good clue can be obtained from the serial number – 210,642 means precisely what you think it means – your certificate is not alone.

The five value determinants of condition, rarity, age, signature, and attractiveness are all key factors to consider when adding a new piece to your collection. Throughout the chapter we have stressed the importance of not being too influenced by any one feature – always consider certificates in their particular context and make your assessment accordingly.

All the fun of the fair transmitted by this fine bearer share in the Paris Gigantic Wheel & Varieties Co. Ltd.

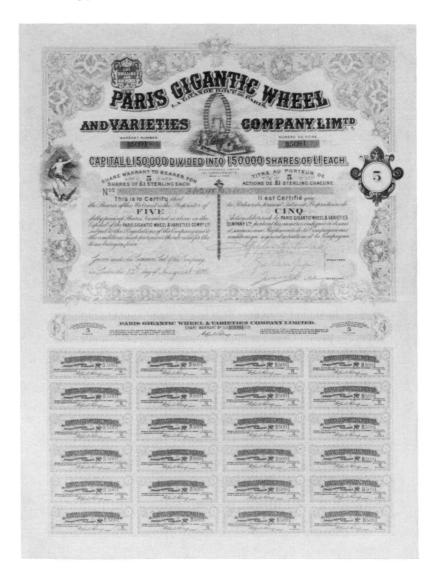

LOOKING AFTER A COLLECTION

Having spent a great deal of time selecting your theme and acquiring the beginnings of a collection, it would be unfortunate to allow lethargy to take hold, for now is the time when you can really get to grips with the development work.

First step – get it insured. The danger is not so much from the local burglar, who probably has never seen a scrip before, but from the goodly elements of fire and water. Most insurance companies are prepared to add the value of a collection, whatever its field, to a normal household policy, unless there are individual items of particularly high value, in which case a listing may be required. An official valuation may be requested but, if your original purchase invoices do not suffice, most dealers will provide a valuation probably at a small charge.

Financial protection does not end with insurance, however, and it is important to realize that bad storage can lead to a steady process of deterioration. Often this is not discovered until you decide to sell and a dealer points out newly scuffed edges, green mould, fresh mouse holes, or worse.

STORAGE

Unless you are one of the investment-only brigade who keep everything in a bank vault or you have them framed and up on your walls, you will probably store your certificates at home and gain pleasure from seeing them occasionally. The sheer size of certain bonds causes problems for even the most dedicated, but, DO NOT BEND. There are three main rules that should be followed:

1 Always lay certificates flat.
2 Keep them dry and avoid temperature extremes.
3 Fully enclose them in an album or other container.

Most large-format bonds and shares will, almost certainly, have spent a significant part of their life folded, thus causing damage to the paper. Halt the deterioration by opening them out and enclose in a protective cover. The see-through storage sheets so far produced are not perfect – finding a balance between an acid-free material and a manageable album page is technically difficult, but work continues in that field. Most albums and sheets sold by reputable dealers are adequate. If you live in a humid environment, allow air to circulate amongst the collection and avoid piling plastic sheets on top of one another.

REPAIR AND CLEANING

Like any kind of restoration work, 'paper conservation' is a highly-skilled craft. Professional repairs take time and cost money, ranging from £5–£6 for the cleaning of small certificates to over £200 for more complex work. To help you better understand the causes of deterioration, and perhaps alert you to its possible continuation, several features are identified below together with their remedies.

1 *Dirt and stains* Caused by constant handling or being left in dusty areas. Yellowing may result from suphuric acid in the atmosphere and other stains from ink, for example. Most stains can be removed by dry cleaning and washing, allowing for fugitive inks and stamps. Solvents or bleaching may be used for persistent marks.
2 *Unsuitable backings* Certificates may have been pasted into share registers or on to board. These can be removed completely and if the piece is very fragile it can be strengthened with a backing of thin Japanese tissue.
3 *Tears and damaged edges* Usually caused by excessive handling, these can be professionally knitted together and backed by thin tissue.
4 *Creases* Large bonds have often been folded thus weakening the paper and causing splits and tears. Creases can be eased out and pressed and weakened areas may be strengthened.
5 *Missing corners and holes* The crispness of the paper ('sizing') may have been knocked out as a result of age and handling, leaving the paper limp and easily liable to tear. Sizing can be restored by brushing a size of leaf gelatine on to the back of the certificate.

Many bonds and shares have experienced an obviously hard life, and it is often the most rare which incurred greatest damage. Expert repair work, although costly, can enhance the value of an item, but do-it-

A share certificate of 1904 in the Missouri, Kansas & Texas Railway Co. – once part of the Jay Gould empire.

yourself jobs may prove disastrous. A repaired item will never have the same value as an EF or VF piece and it should always be described as having undergone repair when listed in dealers' or auctioneers' catalogues.

A tip for those minor clean-up jobs – it is amazing what can be achieved with a soft eraser lightly applied across the whole certificate. And for the laundrette enthusiast – most shares can be relieved of their backing paper by a twenty minute soak in the bath, but watch out for running signatures (black ink is usually waterproof). Iron from the back through a piece of heavy paper to avoid scorching and shining. Experiments should be limited to less expensive items and is really only recommended for the very careful and dextrous amateur.

FRAMING

Nothing is too expensive to frame (see the National Gallery for examples). There are few of us with either the wall space or the desire to frame a whole collection, but the attractiveness and size of bonds make them ideal candidates for putting behind glass, and one or two well-placed pieces can add considerable character and colour to a home or office.

There are few rules to remember about framing, but nevertheless they are very important. Stress to your framer that he or she *must* use acid-free backing materials and *must not* glue or cut the certificate. Whether you choose normal or non-reflecting glass is a matter of personal taste, but avoid hanging in direct sunlight.

CATALOGUING AND RESEARCH

Keep a careful register of your collection, note prices paid and dates purchased, and record changing auction and dealer prices. Such data will prove useful should you choose to sell at some future date providing a good guide to value. The method and sophistication of cataloguing adopted is very much up to personal choice; whereas some prefer a card index system, others may be satisfied by adapting a standard multi-column cash book. Whatever your approach, a complete set of records will aid your knowledge and interest in developing a collection.

Compared with more developed collector fields, such as stamps and coins, very little published material exists on scripophily. The opportunity for personal research is enormous and can prove to be a fascinating and rewarding experience. Many of us have a secret ambition to put pen to paper and here is a perfect opportunity. Magazines are always seeking new articles and a well-researched and -written piece has every chance of achieving publication. Even if literary fame is not your ambition, researching a collection not only gives pleasure, but also enhances its value.

A well-presented and catalogued collection is always a pleasure to see and with scripophily as your chosen hobby the chance to break new ground is enormous.

HOW AND WHERE TO SELL

Building up a collection can be a long, slow and, probably, enjoyable process. At the time, thoughts of selling may well be far from your mind, but the ability to be able to sell at some future date is most reassuring, particularly when debating whether or not to purchase the more expensive pieces. Many collectors consider the act of selling to be a fundamental part of the collecting hobby. In effect, such people become mini-dealers – buying, selling and exchanging items frequently. Active trade between collectors is always a healthy sign of the strength of a market, and mainly arises for two reasons:

1 A collector's decision to develop a particular theme and thus keen to dispose of non-compatible items in his or her collection.
2 The possibility of a quick profit. A bargain can rarely be resisted and an offer of a quantity of a certificate may well present the purchaser with the chance of covering the cost of one by selling the rest.

There are of course more significant reasons for items being sold, financial need and death, to name but two. This chapter seeks to cover all eventualities, which may be adapted to particular requirements. As with all collecting hobbies, a balance between time and price exists and the following rules have as much application to fine paintings as to bonds and shares:

1 Do not expect to make money or even fully recover your initial outlay by selling less than five years from purchase.
2 Selling in a hurry will always prove disadvantageous. Take a month or so to check out all possibilities.

Before returning to the final act of sale, let us first establish a price.

PUTTING A VALUE ON YOUR COLLECTION

In the first chapter of Part 3, we dealt at some length with the major determinants of value; condition, rarity, age, signature, and attractiveness. Although at the time we were primarily concerned with purchase value, the factors have just as much significance in determining resale value. Without the assistance of an expert, it is perhaps difficult to objectively assess the true quality of your collection, nevertheless, the guidelines provided should be of help in at least categorizing it as 'good', 'average' or 'poor'. For the purposes of this chapter, we assume 'average'.

It was recommended earlier that one of the first tasks of developing a collection was to create, and regularly update, a register in which purchase prices, changing dealer list prices, and auction results should be recorded. From this file two essential pieces of information may be extracted – the initial cost and the average current dealer retail price.

Using these basic figures and applying factors to allow for age of the collection and extremes, a few minor calculations need to be performed to ascertain the level at which you should be prepared to sell. It should be stressed at the outset that this method is not being propounded as a one hundred per cent fail-safe solution – it is merely intended to place an approximate value on a collection built up over a number of years. Fashion trends are ignored and it is assumed that both purchases and sale take place in average market conditions. This is an important qualification; selling in times of deep economic recession may prove impossible and buying in times of hyper-inflation can be over-costly. Having ascertained the initial cost, the next stage is to group purchases into years. Set up your worksheet as in the following example:

AGE	AMOUNT ORIGINALLY SPENT	VALUE/AGE FACTOR	CURRENT VALUE
5 years	£300	2.00	£600
4 years	250	1.46	365
3 years	250	1.00	250
2 years	100	.80	80
1 year	100	.60	60
	£1,000		£1,355

Opposite: *Société Forestière Franco-Australienne. A share certificate of a French company trading with Australia and most unusually it incorporates photographs as illustrations.*

Left: *Napoleon Bonaparte figures prominently on this Los Angeles controlled company – most unusual and quite irrelevant, but no doubt it impressed the punters.*

Below: *Toledo, St Louis & Western Railroad Co., $500 bond, 1900.*

Some explanation is required. In the example, the collection was started five years ago at which time £300 was spent. Over the next four years additions were made, so that by the end of the period a total outlay of £1,000 had been made. Assuming all else equal, the major determinant of current value is the age of the collection. The longer a piece has been held, the greater should be its value; and conversely, the more recently it has been purchased, the less its value as a proportion of cost. The 'value/age factor' in our calculation is designed to quantify the effect of age. Thus, items held for five years may be expected to have a current value of at least twice their original cost, whereas items held for only one year are unlikely to have a value more than sixty per cent of original cost. This seemingly low proportion reflects the inclusion of dealer margins and taxes in the purchase prices. Multiplying the original outlay by the value/age factor produces an indicative current value which, in the example, amounts to £1,355 in total versus the original cost of £1,000.

Once this figure has been calculated it must be compared with the average current dealer retail price. At least three dealers should be consulted in order to iron out extremes. Take sixty per cent of the result and compare with the alternative calculation. The lower of the two figures will then represent the approximate value of your collection in the open market in normal circumstances. Remember, however, no matter how a figure is arrived at technically, in the final analysis, value is what someone is prepared to pay. So who are these potential buyers?

AUCTIONS AND DEALERS

With the increasing sophistication and expertise of the average collector, auction houses have succeeded in cornering a major portion of the antique trade at the expense of traditional dealers. Collectors feel that buying or selling at auction gives them a distinct trade advantage. Usual thinking is that it is cheaper to buy, as that is where dealers buy, and easier to obtain a higher price when selling, as that is where collectors buy. A suspect logic, but nevertheless one which the houses themselves have done much to encourage.

Many of the auction companies have become household names, synonymous with quality and integrity. A position once again encouraged by the houses themselves, despite occasional errors or scandals which appear in the press from time to time. Once the bailiwick of the landed gentry, auction rooms have opened their doors to the world and all clients are welcomed.

Bidding at auction can be an exciting experience, but remember, it is easy to get carried away and pay too high a price; remember also that the buyer is responsible for ascertaining the quality of the goods offered for sale. Most auction houses clearly state this condition in their catalogues; the following quote from a Sotheby catalogue is typical:

> Goods auctioned are usually of some age. All goods are sold with all faults and imperfections and errors of description. Illustrations in catalogues are for identification only. Buyers should satisfy themselves prior to sale as to the condition of each lot and should exercise and rely on their own judgement as to whether the lot accords with its description. Subject to the obligations accepted by Sotheby's under this condition, none of the sellers, Sotheby's, its servants or agents is responsible for errors of description or for the genuineness or authenticity of any lot, no warranty whatever is given by Sotheby's, its servants or agents, or any seller to any buyer in respect of any lot and any express or implied conditions or warranties are hereby excluded.

You have been warned!

Auction houses employ a large number of specialists who are able to provide prospective sellers with estimates of prices likely to be achieved. Such advice is usually given free of charge and once you have gained an initial personal 'feel' of the value of your collection, a visit to an auctioneer is recommended. Auction houses make their money on commissions which are usually only earned if a lot is sold; the more lots they are able to sell an hour, the higher their overall income. Thus they are not interested in offering pieces for which there is no demand.

A great deal of publicity often surrounds the disposal of a private collection at auction; but to warrant such publicity, and indeed to warrant the auctioneer accepting a complete collection for sale, necessitates the seller having a unique and highly valuable collection. Unless this is the case only selected pieces should be auctioned. These pieces should be the unusual or rarer items which could well realize considerably more at auction than from sale to a dealer. Particularly suitable pieces are those relating to a specialized subject – for example, share certificates of early football, golf or cricket clubs, or those with famous signatures.

Left: *Attractive and early share in the Universal Salvage Co., dated 1845.*

Below: *An unusual item from Japan portraying James Watt.*

Care should be taken in choosing which auction houses to use and in which country. There is little point in auctioning early German material in the USA, the market for that field lies in Germany and that is where it will achieve best prices. Certain houses are better for buying than selling: in London, Phillips, Son & Neale fits the former category, and Sotheby's, the latter.

Guidelines for selling at auction are as follows:

1 First get a feel for the value of particular items using the methods explained. This will help determine your reserve price.
2 Select the right material for auction; preferably the unusual or special.
3 Select the right auction house in the right country.
4 Check on any commissions payable by you as a seller.

After an initial visit to the auctioneer and *before* committing anything for sale through that medium, call on your dealer – and not just one dealer, but as many as you have time to visit, and the emphasis is on VISIT. Standard letters through the mail, with or without photocopies, are insufficient. If you want a quick decision, a dealer needs to see the actual items for sale in order to check condition – your physical presence will prompt a fast response, whereas letters can easily be left on the side.

There are several options open to a dealer and he or she may well suggest a combination of methods of disposal so as to maximize your return. The most obvious is to buy outright and although this may not provide you with the highest price, it does have the benefit of immediacy and simplicity. An alternative would be to sell on commission; your bonds would be offered to clients, and on completion of a sale, the proceeds less commission would be paid to you. Commission rates vary amongst dealers, but fifteen to twenty per cent is about the norm. Another alternative is for the dealer to handle the placing with auction houses; he or she is usually more aware of forthcoming auctions throughout the world and better placed than the private collector to select the most appropriate.

A good dealer should always be able to come up with a programme of disposal and discussions with such people can be most helpful. But if dealers and auction houses are not for you, there is always another alternative.

PRIVATE SALE

Successful private sale can often result in achievement of the best prices, but it takes time, patience and, where advertising is involved, money. Apart from selling to friends and acquaintances, there are two approaches:

1 Classified advertising.
2 Sending lists of available items to known collectors.

For classified advertising in England, the following publications are suggested; *Exchange & Mart*, Monday's *Daily Mail*, *Bond & Share Society Newsletter*. In the USA, *Friends of Financial History* is recommended, and in Europe, *Freunde Historische Wertpapiere* and *HP Magazine*.

Lists of known collectors are usually available from your local society – a further reason for joining. Not much else can be added about private sale except to say that it is possibly the hardest way of disposing of a collection.

The major auction houses and dealers can be found opposite.

APPENDICES

MAJOR DEALERS, AUCTION HOUSES, SOCIETIES AND PUBLICATIONS

GREAT BRITAIN

Dealers:

G. K. R. Bonds, P.O. Box 1, Kelvedon CO5 9EH (Tel. 0376 71138)

W. H. Collectables, Westcombe House, 56/58 Whitcomb Street, London WC2 (Tel. 01 930 5241)

Herzog Hollender Phillips & Co., 9 Old Bond Street, London W1X 3TA (Tel. 01 493 7681)

London Scripophily Centre Ltd, 5 Albemarle Street, London W1 (Tel. 01 493 4292)

Scripophily International Promotions, Selbourne Suite, Westbrooke House, High Street, Alton GU34 1HB (Tel. 0420 83335)

R. M. Smythe & Co., Grand Buildings, Suite 352, Trafalgar Square, London WC2N 5HB (Tel. 01 930 2887)

Zararing Ltd, 45 Melrose Road, London SW18 (Tel. 01 870 0278)

Auction Houses:

Phillips Son & Neale, Blenstock House, 7 Blenheim Street, London W1Y 0AS (Tel. 01 629 6602)

Sotheby Parke Bernet & Co., 34–35 New Bond Street, London W1 (Tel. 01 493 8080)

Societies and publications:

Bond & Share Society, B. Mills, 56 The Avenue, Tadworth, Surrey KT20 5DE

Old Bond Times, Herzog Hollender Phillips & Co.

EUROPE

Dealers:

* Christine Schlacher, Berggasse 8/17, A–1090 Vienna, Austria (Tel. 0222 34 61 74)

* Numistoria, 49 Rue Vivienne, 75002 Paris, France (Tel. Paris 75002)

* Iegor de Saint Hippolyte, 25 Rue Sarrette, 75014 Paris, France (Tel. Paris 75014)

* F. Kuhlmann, Seilerstrasse 15/17, 300 Hannover 1 Germany (Tel. 4911–8093191)

Hans-Joachim Weber, Hohenzollernstrasse 23–25, Postfach 8634, Dusseldorf 1, Germany (Tel. 0211–357581).

Erstes Wertpapier-Antiquariat, Wittener Strasse 78, 4630 Bochum, Germany (Tel. 0234–331596)

Clubex Sten Erickson, Fack S–10432, Stockholm 19, Sweden

Peo Mynt & Frimarken AB., Drottninggatan 29, Box 16245, S–10325, Stockholm, Sweden (Tel. 08–211210)

Galerie Sevogel, Sevogelstrasse 76, 4052 Basel, Switzerland (Tel. 061–422659)

Freddy Tschumi, Rue de la Dime 94, CH–2000, Neuchatel, Switzerland (Tel. 038–331206)

Auction houses:

Auktionshaus Peter Ineichen, CF Meyer-Strasse 14, 8002 Zurich, Switzerland

* See also above

Societies:

Osterreichischer Club Fur Historische Wertpapiere, Albert Beroncau, Investors Club, Schottengasse 4, A–1010, Vienna, Austria

Svenska Foreningen for Historiska Vardepapper, Box 16246, S–10325, Stockholm, Sweden

Verenging Verzamelaars Oude Fondsen, P.O. Box 17071, Amsterdam, Holland

Publications:

Historische Wertpapiere, Goethestrasse 23, 6000 Frankfurt 1, Germany

HP Magazine fur Historische Wertpapiere, Postfach 172, CH–3000 Bern 15, Switzerland

USA

Dealers:

Applegate & Applegate, 1410 Stallion Lane, West Chester, Pennsylvania 19380 (Tel. 215 6928034)

Buttonwood Galleries, P.O. Box 1006, Throggs Neck Station, New York, N.Y. 10465 (Tel. 212 823 1523)

Criswells, Route 2, Box 1085, Ft McCoy, Florida 32637 (Tel. 904 685 2287)

George H. La Barre Galleries Inc., P.O. Box 27, Hudson, New Hampshire 03051 (Tel. 603 882 2411)

BIBLIOGRAPHY

Compiling a first book on scripophily has necessitated drawing on a wide variety of reference books. Most are listed below and those which the collector may find of specific benefit have been asterisked.

Arnold, David *Britain, Europe and the World 1871–1971* Edward Arnold
Austin, K. A. *The Lights of Cobb & Co.* Angus & Robertson
Bagwell, Philip S. *The Transport Revolution from 1770* B. T. Batsford Ltd
* Bond and Share Society of Great Britain *Newsletter*
Boulton, W. H. *The Pageant of Transport Through the Ages* Blom
Cipolla, Carlo M. *The Fontana Economic History of Europe* 1980
* Council of Foreign Bondholders, 1980 Annual Report
* Criswell, Grover C. *Confederate and Southern State Bonds* 1979
Davies, P. N. *The Trade Makers* (Elder Dempster in West Africa 1852–1972) George Allen & Unwin
* Drumm & Henseler *Old Securities – Chinese Bonds & Shares* 1976
*   *Old Securities – Russian City Bonds* 1981
                  Old Securities – Russian Railway Bonds 1979
* Encyclopaedia Britannica
* *Friends of Financial History Magazine,* R. M. Smythe & Co. New York
Frostick, Michael *A History of Motors & Motoring Vol 2* Haynes
Hatch, Alder *American Express 1850–1950* Doubleday & Co. Inc. 1950
Kettle, Michael *The Allies and the Russian Collapse* Vol 7 Andre Deutsch
May, Robin *The Gold Rushes* William Luscombe 1977
Money, D. C. *South America* U.T.P. 1972
Nock, O. S. *World Atlas of Railways*
Rosenthal, Eric *On 'Charge Through the Years – A History of Share Dealing in South Africa'* Flesch Financial Publications 1968
Stock Exchange Year Books

EXAMPLES OF AUCTION PRICES REALIZED (Note currency)

ITEM	AUCTION HOUSE AND DATE	AMOUNT (excluding premium)
Imperial Chinese Government 4½% Gold Loan, issued by Deutsch-Asiatische Bank, £500 denomination, 1898	Stanley Gibbons 14 September 1979	£14,000
Hispano Suiza Motor Co., Ptas. 500, 1918	Christie's 13 December 1979	£310
Stockton & Darlington Railway Co. £25 preference share, 1858	Phillips 21 February 1980	£520
Australian Agricultural Co., share certificate £100, 1824	Sotheby's 19 March 1980	£320
Paris Gigantic Wheel & Varieties Co. Ltd, share certificate, 1898	Sotheby's 19 March 1980	£65
Canal Maritime de Corinthe, share certificate, 1887	Sotheby's 19 March 1980	£32
City of Nicolaiev 5% bond 1st issue, £100, 1912	Sotheby's 19 March 1980	£65
Blue Ridge RR. Co. 7% bond for £200, 1869	Sotheby's 15 September 1980	£60
The Albany Railway, share certificate, 1875	R. M. Smythe & Co. 16 October 1980	$98
The Irish Republic, unissued $10 bond of 1860s	R. M. Smythe & Co. 16 October 1980	$550
New York & Harlem RR. certificate for 1,000 shares signed by Commodore Vanderbilt, 1863	R. M. Smythe & Co. 16 October 1980	$3,000
Thames & Severn Canal Navigation Co., unissued share of c. 1783 on vellum	Sotheby's 23 March 1981	£85
Société Nouvelle des Automobiles Martini, 1911	Peter Incichen, Zurich 3 April 1981	Sw. Fr. 350
The Denver & Rio Grande RR. Co., 1893 share certificate	Peter Ineichen, Zurich 3 April 1981	Sw. Fr. 70
Buenos Ayres Lacroze Tramways 5% £100 bond, 1913	Peter Ineichen, Zurich 3 April 1981	Sw. Fr. 90
American Express Co., signed by Wells & Fargo, 1865	R. M. Smythe & Co. 14 October 1981	$375
Chinese Hukuang Railway £100 bond issued by US Banks, 1911	R. M. Smythe & Co. 14 October 1981	$135
Liverpool & Manchester Railway Co., 1828 share certificate on vellum	Sotheby's 18 March 1982	£1,500

INDEX

Figures shown in *italic type* refer to illustration captions.